Up the Income Ladder

Up the Income Ladder

GENERATE MORE INCOME IN RETIREMENT

William Robert Parrott

Copyright © 2016 William Robert Parrott
All rights reserved.

ISBN: 1533178739
ISBN 13: 9781533178732
Library of Congress Control Number: 2016907931
CreateSpace Independent Publishing Platform
North Charleston, South Carolina

To Tonya and Hannah, my two best investments.

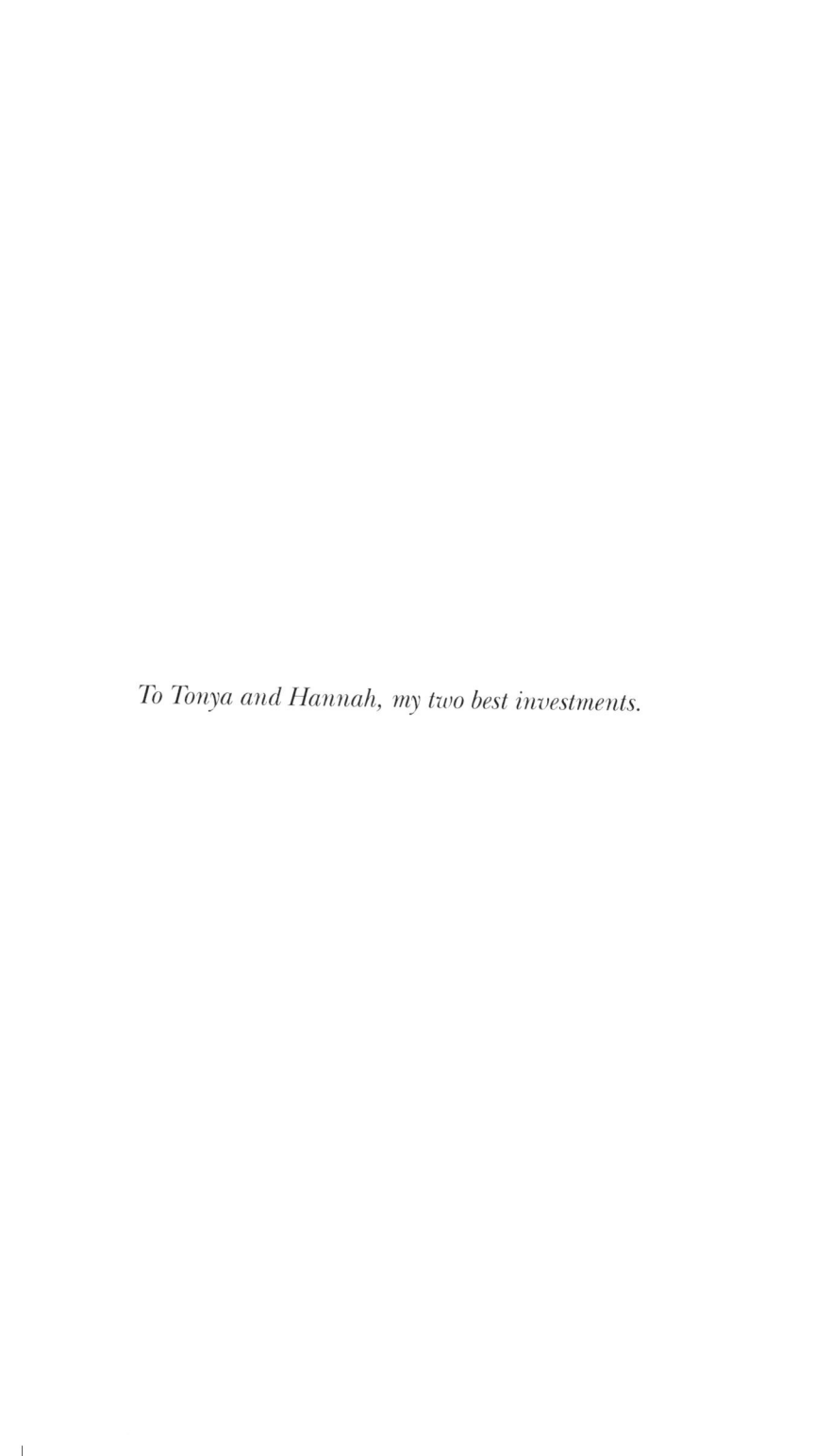

Acknowledgments

I'd like to thank my lovely wife, Tonya, for her love, encouragement, and editing; my amazing daughter, Hannah, for her never-ending love and support for my wild and crazy dreams; my parents, Bill and Barbara Parrott; my sister and brother-in-law, Katie and Jason Rose; my aunt and uncle, Margaret and Dennis Page; my aunt, Virginia Snyder; and my in-laws, Saundra and Duncan Murray, all for their editing advice.

Table of Contents

	Acknowledgments	vii
Chapter 1	Giving	1
Chapter 2	The Beginning	4
Chapter 3	How Much Income Do You Need?	9
Chapter 4	Retirement	17
Chapter 5	Financial Plan	21
Chapter 6	Risk versus Reward	26
Chapter 7	Asset Allocation	37
Chapter 8	Debt	43

Chapter 9	Estate Planning for Income	45
Chapter 10	Systematic Withdrawal Plan	52
Chapter 11	Required Minimum Distribution	56
Chapter 12	Interest Rates	59
Chapter 13	Funds	62
Chapter 14	Bond Definitions	68
Chapter 15	The Bond Ladder	74
Chapter 16	Investments	79
Chapter 17	Cash	81
Chapter 18	Certificates of Deposits	85
Chapter 19	US Treasuries	89
Chapter 20	Municipal Bonds	94
Chapter 21	Corporate Bonds	98
Chapter 22	Stocks	101
Chapter 23	Options	110

Chapter 24 Preferred Stocks · · · · · · · · · · · · · · · · · · · 115

Chapter 25 Real-Estate Investment Trusts · · · · · · · · 118

Chapter 26 Annuities · 121

Chapter 27 Benchmarks · 126

Chapter 28 Portfolio Construction · · · · · · · · · · · · · 131

Chapter 29 Mr. Market · 136

Chapter 30 Money Management · · · · · · · · · · · · · · · 140

Chapter 31 DIY Investing · 142

Chapter 32 Advisors · 146

Chapter 33 The Mechanics of Moving Money · · · · · 150

Chapter 34 Summary · 155

CHAPTER 1
GIVING

Honor the Lord with your wealth, with the firstfruits of all your crops; then your barns will be filled to overflowing, and your vats will brim over with new wine.
—PROVERBS 3:9–10

In 2012 I went on a mission trip to Nicaragua with some mighty men from my church. On one of our stops, we went to visit a small town in the hills just outside of Managua. This village had little, if anything, of what you'd consider necessary for living. A dirt road led to makeshift shanties nestled among the coffee trees. We were distributing bags of food, which consisted mostly of rice. While handing out food, I met a man who was well into his nineties. I had the privilege of walking him back to his home. It was a five-minute walk down the road from the three-walled church located in the center of the little town.

He lived in an abandoned coffee-bean storage room. He had a rundown bed and a stack of firewood in the corner. His walls were black from the smoke from fires he built to keep warm at night. His front door was nothing more than a few pieces of wood secured by a fragile padlock.

> *The king will reply, Truly I tell you, whatever you did for one of the least of these brothers and sisters of mine, you did for me.*
> —MATTHEW 25:40

I was moved by where and how he lived. He clearly didn't have any financial resources. The next day he was sitting in the front row in the three-walled church, smiling and singing. When it was time for the offering, he was the first to stand up and put his tithe in the passing bowl. He did it with a smile on his face and peace in his heart. While he gave only a few cents, this incredible nonagenarian knew the power of giving. He knew he was blessed and his offering would, in turn, bless the church and the people of his village. It was very humbling to watch this man give a large percentage of his net worth to help others.

It may seem odd to open a book about generating income with a story about giving money away. After all, it is counterintuitive to give something away in order to get more in return. Yet, however, odd it sounds, the amazing thing about giving money away is that you truly do end up receiving more in return.

If you're reading this book, you probably have investments and income opportunities most people around the world can only dream of. Your wealth allows you to give comfortably (or uncomfortably) to help others who are in need of resources such as food, clothing, shelter, and water. The amazing thing about giving money away is you'll end up receiving more in return. The return on your "investment" may be financial, but it's more likely spiritual. In fact, there is only one place in the Bible where God tells us to test Him, and it happens to be on the subject of giving which is the only time in the Bible God asks you to test him. It sounds serious.

> *"Bring the whole tithe into the storehouse, that there may be food in my house. Test me in this," says the LORD Almighty, "and see if I will not throw open the floodgates of heaven and pour out so much blessing that there will not be room enough to store it."*
> —MALACHI 3:10

I hope this book not only helps you to add wealth to your storehouse, but also inspires you to use some of it to help others live a fuller life.

CHAPTER 2

THE BEGINNING

Let there be light
GENESIS *1:3*

As people near or enter retirement, generating investment income becomes a high priority. In this book, we will explore ways to generate more income from existing investments, such as stocks, bonds, and cash. The investment strategies are simple and easy to employ, requiring minimal cost. While there are hundreds of income-producing ideas, our primary focus will be on publicly traded investments.

As we hunt for yield, we should take comfort in the fact God is in control and has a plan for us all. The Bible is filled with verses about God providing for our needs. We are told repeatedly to have no fears or worries, because God will never leave us nor forsake us. These words are powerful and comforting. God isn't timid, nor should we be when we pursue life and investing opportunities:

> *For the Spirit God gave us does not make us timid, but gives us power, love and self-discipline.*
> —2 TIMOTHY 1:7

The challenge for most retirees today is the fact that interest rates are so low. As we pursue a higher rate of income, we have to consider both the safety and growth of our principal. After retiring, we may live for another twenty, thirty, or even forty years, so we need assets to meet our needs of today and those of tomorrow. This is a delicate balance, and we want to make sure our investments are positioned correctly to meet these competing goals.

In my years in the business, I've found most investors want more income regardless of the current level of interest rates. When I started as a stockbroker, the typical interest rate on a triple-A-rated tax-free California municipal bond was paying over 7 percent. This meant that if someone invested $100,000 into one of these bonds, the annual income would have been $7,000 per year—tax-free! Today this same bond might bring in $3,000 or less. As good as this deal was, however, when I presented these figures to investors, they wanted to know if they could get 7.25 percent, 7.5 percent or even 8 percent. Although the 7 percent rate was high, investors still wanted more.

At that time, most people didn't realize we were in the midst of a bull market for bonds, meaning interest rates were falling and bond prices were rising. In fact, interest rates had been falling since the early 1980s, and the 7 percent tax-free bond would slowly vaporize to the low rates we see today.

In my early twenties, the telephone was my main means of prospecting. I tried cold calling to generate business on local tax-free or US Treasury bonds. At one point during this time, the thirty-year US Treasury bond was paying a guaranteed 8 percent for thirty years.[1] But I couldn't give them away. People were confident interest rates were going to rise again, and they didn't want to lock up their money for thirty years. It's hard to fathom; this was over twenty-five years ago, and if investors bought these bonds, they'd still be enjoying 8 percent income. Today, the interest rate on the thirty-year Treasury bond is 2.65 percent.

With rates as low as they currently are, most individuals want to wait for rates to go back up before investing. I've heard numerous people say rates have been down for so long that at some point, they have to go higher. But interest rates don't *have* to do anything. They can stay at these levels for a long time. To prove this point, let's look at the Japanese overnight interest rate. In December 1973, this rate peaked at 9 percent. In 1995, it went below

---

[1] U.S. Department of the Treasury, Resource Center, https://www.treasury.gov/resource-center/data-chart-center/interest-rates/Pages/Historic-LongTerm-Rate-Data-Visualization.aspx.

UP THE INCOME LADDER

1 percent and is currently negative.[2] Regardless, most people remain convinced interest rates will rise soon.

In the meantime, investors have been leaving money in checking or savings accounts, waiting for those rates to rise as well. They're leaving money—a lot of money—on the table even in this low-interest-rate environment. The cash we hold in our bank accounts today isn't generating income, nor is it growing. Moving cash into another investment may help us generate more income today and provide for our future needs. There are a number of strategies and investments we can take advantage of today to help us generate more income—more on this later.

Another issue affecting retirees today is the loss of the corporate pension plan. A pension plan is now offered by only 24 percent of companies in the S&P 500, down from 60 percent in 1998.[3] These plans have been replaced by the defined contribution plan; the 401(k) plan is the retirement plan now offered by most companies. With a 401(k), you have to decide how much to contribute and how to invest. You're responsible for your own retirement, not your employer.

In addition, Uncle Sam, given its current financial state, may alter your Social Security benefits. This has

---

[2] Trading Economics, Japan Interest Rate 1972 – 2016. http://www.tradingeconomics.com/japan/interest-rate.

[3] *Nearly a quarter of Fortune 500 companies still offer pensions to new hires*, Jonnelle Marte, 9/5/2014. https://www.washingtonpost.com/news/get-there/wp/2014/09/05/nearly-a-quarter-of-fortune-500-companies-still-offer-pensions-to-new-hires/.

already started by extending the full retirement age from sixty-five to sixty-seven.[4]

So what does this mean? For retirees, the pressure to generate our own income has never been greater. In a low-rate, pension less, benefit-free world, we're forced to take more investment risk to make ends meet. We have no choice but to look at different asset classes and investment strategies to generate this lost income. This can also be considered a warning for future generations: start saving *early*.

We need to save early and often, with a focus on long-term growth. We also must strive to be better stewards of our capital. We need to take control of our spending. The less we spend, the more we save; the more we save, the more we have.

In the third verse of the Bible, God says, "Let there be light." He was shining light on the darkness of the world. Just as a flashlight allows you to see the path before you when you are hiking, my hope is to shed some light on your retirement path so you can earn more money from your existing investments.

---

[4] What is the Social Security Retirement Age? National Academy of Social Insurance, https://www.nasi.org/learn/socialsecurity/retirement-age.

CHAPTER 3

HOW MUCH INCOME DO YOU NEED?

Give us today our daily bread.
—MATTHEW 6:11

How much income is enough? How much money do you need? In the Lord's Prayer, the answer is given to us in the form of daily bread: "Give us today our daily bread" (Matthew 6:11). The Lord's Prayer is comforting, and the peace it provides is welcoming. Knowing our daily needs will be met empowers us and brings us joy.

The challenging part for people entering retirement is determining the level of income needed to last a lifetime. We don't want to run out of money at eighty-three if we are going to end up living into our nineties.

The two questions I'm asked most often by people are, "How much income will I need?" and "How long will it last?" The first question is easier to answer than the second. You will need income to cover your annual expenses at a minimum. If you generate two dollars in income and spend one, life is good. If you generate two dollars in income and spend three, life is bad. I recommend you immediately begin tracking your household expenses. The amount of income you'll need to generate in retirement will be driven in large part by your expenses.

A strong budget will help you drill down on your monthly and annual expenses. It's likely your expenses won't change dramatically from your working years to your golden years, so the amount of money you need in retirement will probably be about the same as it was while you were working. While the dollar amount may stay the same, however, the spending categories will change. For example, instead of putting money into Johnny's college fund, you'll now add it to your travel bucket.

The best way to budget for retirement is to look back at where you have been spending your money. What financial footprints did you leave behind? A deep dive into your spending from the past two or three years will help paint a picture of where your retirement expenses may land. I recommend closely reviewing your checkbook and credit-card statements so you can get a handle on where you've spent your money. You may be surprised at how much money goes out the door without your giving it much thought.

In the course of daily life, it's easy to lose track of how much money you spend on items of no lasting value. I find it interesting to look back at my expenses for the year to see where my money was consumed. For my family it's always a close tie between my trips to Home Depot and my wife's visits to Target. Once you review your spending habits, you'll be able to generate a budget for you and your family. Identifying where your money has been will make it easier for you to adjust your spending.

Can you find a few expenses to prune during your review? As you approach retirement, I recommend doing a budget review every quarter to get a handle on your spending habits. By reducing your expenses, you'll be in a better position to save for retirement. I also suggest increasing your spending budget by 5–10 percent to give yourself a little wiggle room before you retire. You can always come down from this higher number once you get a feel for your retirement spending.

It's not uncommon to see a spike in spending just prior to retirement. This spike could be the result of a number of factors, such as buying a car or remodeling a kitchen.

I've added a black swan, or random event, category to my budget to cover those unexpected events that occur during the course of a year, such as a car repair, home repair, medical expenses, and so on.

In retirement, housing will account for a large part of your annual expenses. According to the Consumer Expenditure Survey,[5] from 2014 to 2015, housing accounted for over 32 percent of a person's budget for those ages sixty-five and older. Even if you don't have a mort-

---

5 Consumer Expenditure Survey, CE 3RD quarter 2014 – 2nd quarter 2015 Table 1300, http://www.bls.gov/cex/22015/midyear/age.pdf.

gage, housing is a huge expense in retirement. Utilities, property taxes, and repairs are constant expenses that attack your budget. Other expenses that take a large part of a retiree's budget are transportation at 15.6 percent, health care at 12.59 percent, and food items at 11.97 percent.

So let's review the original question: How much money do you need for a comfortable retirement? Obviously, if you have annual expenses of $100,000, you'll need more than $100,000 in income to cover your expenses. The income you generate may come from your investments, pension, Social Security, or all of the above. In order to generate $100,000, you may need $2.5 million in assets.

How did I come up with $2.5 million? The magic number in this equation is 4 percent. Why 4 percent? Bill Bengen,[6] a former solo practitioner and registered investment advisor, introduced the investment world to the 4 percent rule. I won't go into the details of his study or analysis, but he found that if you withdraw 4 percent of your assets every year, you should not run out of money. So in the above example, to arrive at $2.5 million, you would divide your expenses by 4 percent ($100,000/.04 = $2,500,000). You could also multiply $100,000 by 25 (the inverse of 4 percent) to get the same result. In this low-interest-rate environment, note that a number of planners have suggested a reduced withdrawal rate of 3 percent of your assets. The important point here is that as long as

---

6 *Journal of Financial Planning, Determining Withdrawal Rates Using Historical Data*, by William P. Bengen, October 1994, http://www.retailinvestor.org/pdf/Bengen1.pdf.

you are withdrawing less than your accounts are earning, you will never run out of money. If you take out 4 percent and your investments are earning 5 percent, your assets are growing at 1 percent.

Let's take a look at a few examples. Assume your annual expenses are $100,000 per year. At $100,000 per year, you need an investment portfolio of $2.5 million earning 4 percent to generate this income ($2,500,000 × .04 = $100,000). This calculation assumes you are living on the income from your investments and not invading your principal.

When you add Social Security into the equation, you will need less in the form of assets. For example, if your Social Security income is $30,000 per year, you can deduct that amount from your $100,000 expense number to get $70,000. This revised figure is what your investments will need to generate. Applying the 4 percent rule to $70,000 gives you $1.75 million ($70,000/.04).

If you have a company pension, your need to generate income from your investments is reduced even further. Let's say you'll receive an annual pension of $20,000. Subtracting out your Social Security and pension payments, the amount of income you need to generate goes down to $50,000 ($100,000 − $30,000 − $20,000 = $50,000). The amount of assets needed to generate $50,000 is now $1.25 million ($50,000/.04).

As you can see, the more passive income you receive in retirement, the fewer assets you'll need to cover your annual expenses. At the beginning of the example, we started with a retiree with no passive income needing an asset base of $2.5 million to generate $100,000 income. In contrast, the retiree who had a pension and was receiving Social Security was able to lower his asset base to $1.25 million and receive the same level of income. I refer to this as a "three-minute financial plan." You can calculate the amount of assets you need for retirement and compare this with your current level of assets to see if you have enough money to retire. Obviously, if you have enough assets to cover your expenses, you can retire at any time—on your terms.

Math can help us answer the second question, which is this: "How long will my money last?" As I mentioned, as long as you're withdrawing less than your accounts are earning, you'll never run out of money. If you start withdrawing more money from your accounts than they generate, you run the risk of running out of money. For example, if you retire with $1 million in your 401(k) and you decide to withdraw 10 percent a year ($100,000) from an account earning 5 percent, your retirement nest egg will only last fifteen years. The duration of your money will also depend on how much money you have saved, your age, your expenses, how your investments are allocated, as well as your health and lifestyle characteristics.

Let's pay another visit to the three-minute financial plan. I've included a table to calculate the level of assets you will need to cover your expenses. A forty-year-old with $50,000 in annual expenses will need $2.3 million at retirement. The inflation rate of 2.5 percent will increase her annual expenses from $50,000 to $92,697 at age sixty-five. Applying the 4 percent rule to her inflation-adjusted expense number (divide by .04 or multiply by 25) will give her $2.3 million ($92,697 × 25).

You can identify your asset number from the table below. Use the inflation factor nearest your age to get the future value of your expenses. Once you have this number, multiply it by 25 for your assets needed in retirement.

Age	Inflation Factor	Expenses Today	Future Value Calculation	Multiple	Assets Needed
40	1.85	$50,000	$92,500	25	$2,312,500
45	1.64			25	
50	1.45			25	
55	1.28			25	
60	1.13			25	
65	1			25	

In the three-minute financial plan, we know the inputs for your age, expenses or income, working years, and current assets. From these items we can determine how much money you'll need to save monthly or annually to reach your goal. The model will also tell us what rate of interest or growth you'll need to earn to achieve your goal.

Going back to our previous example, let's say she has saved $200,000 by age forty and is making the maximum contribution of $18,500 to her company 401(k). We know her asset goal is $2.3 million. She'll need to earn 7.14 percent per year for twenty-five years to reach her asset goal. A long-term rate of 7.14 percent is fairly aggressive, so she will need to own more stocks than bonds to reach her goal. Her allocation to reach this target would probably suggest 75 percent in stocks and 25 percent in bonds and cash. If she is able to save an additional $5,000 per year, she'll need to generate a return of 6.42 percent. The return number has dropped because she's able to save more money. The more she saves, the less her account will need to earn.

As we have demonstrated here, the three-minute financial plan will tell you quickly whether you are on track to meet your retirement needs. This plan can help set the framework for the assets you'll need to reach your goal.

Let's change the parameters a tad and consider a fifty-five-year-old man who wants to retire in ten years. He has $100,000 in annual expenses and $2 million in the bank. His expenses in ten years will become $128,008. His needed asset level is $3,200,211 ($128,008 × 25). Plugging these numbers into the equation, we see that he will need to earn a rate of 4.08 percent, which is very conservative. Because of this, he can own more bonds than stocks. An allocation of 75 percent in bonds and 25 percent in stocks would be typical for his profile.

How much is enough, and how long will it last? As you just read, we can quickly determine this with a few inputs on a calculator or in an Excel spreadsheet. Once you are able to answer these questions based on your own situation, you'll be in a position to make adjustments immediately, and then going forward, you can review and update your plan as needed. The three-minute financial plan can help you to quickly get your retirement on track.

CHAPTER 4

Retirement

*Therefore do not worry about tomorrow,
for tomorrow will worry about itself.*
—Matthew 6:34

When should you retire? Today, tomorrow, never? The answer involves both emotional and financial considerations. The financial part of retirement is fairly easy. If you have enough money to cover your expenses, you can retire at any time regardless of your age. The age at which you obtain these assets could come at any time, especially if you have been a strong saver and a solid investor. The math, for some, does not really help determine when to retire. People like to work or feel the need to continue working long after they've amassed a retirement nest egg to provide for their needs.

The emotional side of retirement is harder to factor into your retirement equation. Walking away from a career you've held for twenty, thirty, or even forty years isn't easy. You have to prepare yourself emotionally for retirement by considering the following questions:

- What will I do in retirement?
- Where will I live?
- How will I spend my time?
- Will I be needed?
- Will I volunteer?
- Could I travel the world?
- Could I learn a new skill?
- Will I move to where my children live?
- Could I golf?
- Could I fish?
- Could I serve?

These are important questions to answer, and you will need to answer them and more before you can transition into retirement.

Moving from work to retirement is similar to jumping over a six-inch, one-hundred-mile-deep crevasse. One hundred miles is a long way down, but you know you can make the six-inch leap to the other side. I've worked with a number of people who've made the six-inch leap from work to retirement, and all of them made it to the other side. I have yet to see one of these individuals jump back to work because they are not enjoying retirement. My clients who have retired say they are busier and happier than ever and wish they'd have done it sooner.

I once worked with a gentleman who gave his employer his notice to retire. Because he had worked for his employer for many years and was one of their key executives, he had to give his employer a lengthy notice before leaving the company. Before doing so, he wanted to go through the financial-planning process to make sure his assets would last throughout retirement. We ran a number of scenarios, and all of them returned the same result: he could afford to retire. He'd come back to me with best- and worst-case scenarios, and every time we got the same answer: he would have a long and comfortable retirement. His challenge was not on the financial side of the equation but the emotional side. His assets were more than sufficient to meet his needs. Once he came to grips with the financial side of his retirement, he was ready to accept the emotional side.

Controlling risk is a very important factor for meeting your income needs. Too little risk and you can potentially run out of money; too much risk and you could expose yourself to unjust market swings that take big chunks out of your nest egg. The best way to control risk exposure is through your allocations to stocks, bonds, and cash. An account heavily weighted to bonds will be more conservative than an account owning a number of stocks. The larger allocation to bonds will be beneficial in the short term and during market corrections. In the long term, you'll need to have more exposure to stocks. The account with a larger allocation to stocks will outpace the conservative account over time.

Finally, do you want to leave assets to your children or grandchildren? Do you want to endow your alma mater or give money to your church? If you're thinking in generational terms, then view your assets as perpetual holdings with assets you never intend to sell. In this case, your exposure to stocks will be much higher than one who plans to bounce their last check when they die.

CHAPTER 5

Financial Plan

> *"For I know the plans I have for you,"*
> *declares the LORD, "plans to prosper*
> *you and not to harm you, plans to*
> *give you hope and a future."*
> —JEREMIAH 29:11

Do you need a financial plan before you retire? Of course! This is your road map to retirement; not only will it help guide your financial success, but it will also help lead you through the retirement maze. A financial plan is important, but just as important is your journey toward the completed financial plan. As you compile your financial data, you'll discover what's important about money and retirement to you and your family. Your dollars will follow your heart's desires. The numbers in the plan will tell you if you are on the right track. The plan will confirm whether you can or cannot retire. Your plan will help change the discussion of what you need to do to get ready for your retirement.

If you're on pace to retire, you should make sure a portion of your assets are protected prior to retirement to avoid any unnecessary risk. In 2007 a number of people could've retired but didn't because they weren't aware of how much money they had in their accounts or what level of income they could generate from their investments. Had these individuals completed a financial plan, they may have been better prepared to retire or at least reduce their risk exposure. Unfortunately, in 2008 the Dow, S&P 500, and NASDAQ each lost over 40 percent of their market value.

If your plan delivers less than good news, it's time for you to amend your retirement thinking. Do you need to save more or spend less? Do you need to adjust your retirement spending numbers? Do you need to work a few more years? Do you need to mix up your investment allocation?

A plan delivering bad news isn't the worst thing in the world. The financial plan is similar to a photo. It's a moment in time. Once you have the answers to your plan, you can make necessary changes so your retirement dreams become reality. This should be no different than going to the doctor and learning that you need to start taking better care of yourself. Most likely you will take corrective measures to live a healthier lifestyle. You'll make the necessary adjustments so you can live a long and happy life.

Can you imagine never going to see a doctor or dentist? The thought would not cross your mind. You visit the doctor and dentist to make sure all is well with your health.

Yet this is not how investors approach investing. They ignore a friendly visit to their financial planner. A well-constructed financial plan will help improve your situation and make you feel better about your coming retirement.

In the early nineties, I worked with a couple in Pasadena as they were approaching retirement. We constructed a thorough retirement spending plan. The plan showed them they were well ahead of their spending target for retirement. Not long after we had completed the analysis, I received a call from the wife. She wanted to buy a new car. She asked if she could afford a new car as a result of the plan we had just completed. I told her she could buy two. I didn't hesitate with my answer because I knew where all their money was and what it meant for them in the long run. The plan gave her a sense of comfort knowing she could buy a car without derailing their retirement plans. This is one of the many benefits of working with a financial planner.

A key piece to your financial plan is the investment policy statement (IPS).[7] It's a road map for your investments and how they should be structured to meet your financial-planning goals. Your IPS should cover the following:

- Time horizon - What is your time horizon for your investment strategy?
- Investment type – Will you own mutual funds, index funds or individual investments?

---
[7] *How to Create a Client Investment Policy Statement*, Roger Wohlner, updated 10/13/2015. http://www.investopedia.com/articles/financial-advisors/101315/how-create-client-investment-policy-statement.asp.

- Investment sectors – Will you own investments across sectors or will you focus on a few like healthcare, energy or financials?
- Quality of investments – Will your investments have high ratings, low ratings or a combination?
- Asset allocation – What percentage of your assets will be in stocks, bonds and cash?
- Review process – How often will you meet with your advisor?
- Fee schedule – What will your annual fee be?

The IPS is commonly used by institutional investors because they have to answer to shareholders or directors. It guides their investment policy and helps protect them against irate shareholders or directors. Most importantly, it keeps them on track.

As an individual investor, you don't have to answer to anyone but yourself. But the IPS will help you stay focused as you successfully navigate the investment world.

Next you'll need to consider an income-distribution or withdrawal plan. Here are a few items to address:

- How will you handle the withdrawal of your assets?
- Which investments will you sell first?
- How much income do you need from each account?
- Will you take a flat dollar amount or a percentage of your assets?

The distribution plan will help with your monthly and annual spending. It will outline when and how much money you should withdraw from your accounts. This policy, along with your financial plan and investment policy statement, will keep you grounded as you continue to manage your assets for a lifetime of enjoyment.

With your plan in place, how often should you review it? An annual review will work well. The best time do so is near your birthday. As you become another year older and wiser, you can take a moment to reflect on the past year. The birthday review will give you a calendar date you shouldn't forget. Alternatively, you can review your plan around life events such as a marriage, birth of a child, new job, or retirement.

This brings to a close the financial-planning section of this book. As you can see, planning involves more than just numbers. What you've actually done is create a life plan for both accumulation and distribution.

CHAPTER 6
RISK VERSUS REWARD

> *"Be strong and courageous. Do not be afraid or terrified because of them, for the LORD your God goes with you; he will never leave you nor forsake you."*
> —DEUTERONOMY 31:6

Bulls make money, bears make money, and pigs get slaughtered. This is an old Wall Street axiom reminding people not to be greedy, and it may lead you to ask yourself how much risk you are willing to take to achieve your financial goals. Quantifying risk is difficult and often cannot be done until we find ourselves in the middle of a financial storm, such as the stock-market corrections of 2000 or 2008.

The risk tolerance of most investors in 1999 or 2007, just prior to the stock-market collapse, was probably pretty high. After all, the market was rising. When it finally corrected (dropped 10 percent or more), these same investors' risk tolerance most likely dropped accordingly.

In order to determine an investor's risk tolerance, I ask the following questions:

- How did you act during the Great Recession in 2008?
- What did you do with your investments?
- Did you sell your investments and move your money to cash, or did you buy more stocks?

A more conservative investor will sell at a time like this, for fear of losing more. In contrast, an aggressive investor will buy stocks while the market is on its way down. Knowing what type of investor you are will help in the construction of your portfolio. A conservative investor will likely have a diversified portfolio of investments covering many different securities and sectors. A more aggressive investor is probably comfortable to concentrate their investments into fewer holdings. Now, if you have no idea what happened in 2008 or do not know what I am referring to, you definitely need an advisor!

Most people know the saying, "Don't put all your eggs in one basket." In other words, diversify. Put the "eggs" you have in multiple baskets, and you will be protected from a catastrophe. On the other hand, Mark Twain said, "Put all your eggs in one basket and watch the basket." Twain's quote is all about concentration. Basically, if your goal is to preserve wealth, you should diversify your investments. If your goal is to create wealth, you should concentrate your investments.

A concentrated plan works well if you pick the right stock at the right time. An early investor in Apple, Berkshire Hathaway, or Coca-Cola has likely done well over time.

If you happen to concentrate your investment in the wrong company, your results will be drastically different. An investor (speculator) in Enron or WorldCom had a much different outcome with his or her concentrated bet. The individuals putting all their eggs in these two companies were left with a whole lot of nothing.

If you're fortunate enough to find one company appreciating substantially, go all in. It's likely most investors will feel more comfortable with a diversified portfolio of stocks, bonds, and cash. The diversification investment program is a much better experience for most investors.

Investors frequently look for a home run every time they step up to the plate to purchase a new stock. These investors want to double or triple their money overnight. Investors want to know what stock is hot right now—where can they make the most money today!

Don't get me wrong. If I purchased a stock and it doubled or tripled overnight, I'd be extremely pleased. The first time this happened to me was in 1993, when I purchased forty-three shares of Dell. At that time, Dell was a little-known computer company in Round Rock, Texas, making money hand over fist. My money doubled overnight, and I sold it not long after I bought it. I thought I was a stock-market genius. Unfortunately, my euphoria was short lived; Dell stock continued to climb and reached insane heights. Not only was I too naïve to hold on to this thoroughbred of a stock, but I also didn't bother to get back in either. The stock continued to climb and created a legion of Dellionaires.

Two of my favorite baseball players of all time are Tony Gwynn and Rod Carew. Gwynn and Carew made a career of hitting singles and doubles, and on occasion, they'd knock one out of the park. These two masters of hitting just wanted to put a little wood on the ball and get it in play. You can employ this same strategy with your investments. If you always swing for the fence, you'll strike out a lot. While you wait for a home run, you can hit singles and doubles, collecting dividend income. Dividends will keep you moving forward while waiting for the principal portion of your assets to increase.

Stock Market Risk

Risk is the result of your investment choices and is something you can control. When people refer to risk in investing, they're mostly referring to an investment that has lost value or principal. Market risk is a market decline in your investments, and it exposes you to the rotations of the stock and bond markets. The more money you have invested in the stock market; the more money you can make or lose. If your allocation to stocks is 100 percent, you are exposing yourself to a lot of volatility.

According to Morningstar's 2015 Ibbotson SBBI Classic Yearbook,[8] the best one-year return for large-company stocks was 53.99 percent in 1933; the worst loss was 43.34 percent in 1931. To reduce your risk of falling stock prices, you can add bonds and cash to your portfolio. For example, a portfolio of 50 percent large-company stocks and 50 percent long-term government bonds would have reduced your loss. The best year for this portfolio was 1995, with a one-year return of 34.71 percent. The worst year was 1931 with a drop of 24.70 percent.

To demonstrate, consider a portfolio made up of 100 percent stock. In 2008, this portfolio would have lost 37 percent. Now consider a portfolio with an allocation of 50 percent stocks and 50 percent bonds; in that same year, it would have lost only 9.72 percent. Owning more bonds and cash will reduce the loss of your investments in the short term and the allocation of stocks, bonds, and cash will determine your rate of return and risk level both in the short and long term.

Let's look at the performance of stocks and bonds during a few famous periods—1987, 2000, and 2008.[9] Most investors will remember the stock-market crash of 1987, where the stock market dropped 508 points on October 19, 1987. That plunge resulted in a one-day loss of 22.61 percent. This decline was terrifying in speed and magnitude. However, the year actually ended with a 5.25 percent gain in large-company stocks. Long-

---

8 *Market Results for Stocks, Bonds, Bills and Inflation 1926 – 2014.* Morningstar ® Ibbotson®SBBI® 2015 Classic Yearbook, page 49.
9 *Market Results for Stocks, Bonds, Bills and Inflation 1926 – 2014.* Morningstar ® Ibbotson®SBBI® 2015 Classic Yearbook, page 42.

term government bonds lost only 2.71 percent in 1987. In 2000, large-company stocks fell 9.10 percent, which was followed by a drop in 2001 of 11.88 percent. They fell again in 2002, this time 22.20 percent. In contrast the long-term US government bonds during these three years were up 21.48 percent in 2000, 3.7 percent in 2001, and 17.84 percent in 2002. In 2008 large-company stocks declined yet again, this time by 37 percent, while long-term government bonds rose 25.87 percent.[10]

The case for diversification is clearly imbedded in these numbers. A portfolio of stocks and bonds will help reduce your risk when compared to a portfolio of 100 percent stocks.

Bond Market Risks

Bonds and fixed income investments carry their own issues. While adding them to your portfolio will help reduce your risk of a stock-market correction, you need to be aware of interest-rate risk. Bonds will not fare well if interest rates rise because the principal portion of the bond goes down. Imagine a see-saw in a park: when one side rises, the other side falls. There is an inverse relationship between interest rates and bond prices. The more money you have in bonds, the more you'll be exposed to interest-rate risk.

I once worked with two gentlemen in Pasadena who wanted to buy California tax-free municipal bonds, regardless of the maturity. Because thirty-year bonds would

---

10 Ibid.

generate the most income and they didn't care about interest-rate risk, this was the option they chose. One thing that did surprise me about their thirty-year bond purchases is they were both in their eighties! Their strategy is rare and unique in constructing a bond portfolio. Most investors who add bonds to their account will own a diversified portfolio of short, intermediate and long term bonds.

If you construct a portfolio of all bonds and cash, you run the risk of running out of money in retirement. In a low-interest-rate environment, it's not possible to generate the returns you'll need for long-term growth. This is called longevity risk, and it refers to you outliving your assets. Retirees can get too conservative in retirement by placing a high percentage of their money in cash, CDs, and bonds, which exposes them to both inflation and longevity risk. With improvements in health care, longevity risk is a new component to factor into retirement planning. How do you combat longevity risk? The best way to offset this risk is to own investments that will grow over time, such as stocks and real estate.

Inflation Risk

The loss of purchasing power, or inflation risk, is another battle we must wage. From 1926 to 2014, inflation averaged 3 percent.[11] For example, say you are generating income of $1,000 per month, and the inflation rate is 3

---
11 *Market Results for Stocks, Bonds, Bills and Inflation 1926 – 2014.* Morningstar ® Ibbotson®SBBI® 2015 Classic Yearbook, page 293.

UP THE INCOME LADDER

percent. Your inflation-adjusted income will drop to $553 over twenty years. This is a drop of over 44 percent in your purchasing power. Inflation risk and longevity risk are close cousins. A rise in inflation for individuals on a fixed income is a real challenge.

In a world where the cost of goods is getting more expensive, it's going to be difficult to maintain your standard of living as you age. Need proof? Look no further than the price of the US postage stamp. In 1972 a first-class stamp was six cents. In 1972 I could mail sixteen letters for one dollar. Today I can mail two. The price of a first-class stamp has increased 716 percent from 1972 for an average annual increase of 4.88 percent.

Not long ago, the company maintaining the vending machines in my office building raised the prices on all snacks. The increase was modest—twenty-five cents on most items. I didn't think twice when I bought had to pay $1.25 rather than $1.00 for my bag of peanut M&M's. Initially, the price increase was a nonevent, but then I considered the percentage increase—25 percent!

Can you imagine if your annual expenses increased by 25 percent? That would mean paying $125,000 a year rather than $100,000. If your mortgage payment is $2,000 per month and the bank increases it by 25 percent, your new payment is $2,500. Or consider your shiny new car with a payment of $500 per month; a 25 percent increase would mean your payment is now $625.

As we determined earlier, if your expenses in retirement are going to be $100,000 per year, you need about $2.5 million in assets ($100,000 × 25 or $100,000/.04). However, inflation causes us to have to revisit these figures. The 25 percent increase in vending-machine products alone will add $25,000 to your expenses. In all, you will need an extra $625,000 to cover your adjusted expenses, and the assets to needed get you to this amount just jumped from $2.5 million to $3.125 million. That is a lot of M&M's!

Credit Risk

Credit risk refers to the quality of bonds you're purchasing. US Treasuries do not carry any credit risk because they are backed by the full faith and credit of the US government. A US government security is triple-A-rated and is a solid investment for those seeking the ultimate in safety.

Corporate and municipal bonds have ratings ranging from triple-A to D. Bonds rated triple-A are a solid bet and a wise choice; bonds rated D are best to avoid. Be aware, though, that there is an inverse relationship between the credit quality of a bond and the income you will receive. Bonds rated triple-A produce lower income than BB-rated bonds; you are being compensated for taking on more risk.

The bonds you purchase are most likely rated by one of two agencies—Moody's or Standard & Poor's (S&P). The following chart shows their rating categories.

UP THE INCOME LADDER

Moody's	S&P	Meaning
Aaa	AAA	High
Aa1	AA+	Grade
Aa2	AA	
Aa3	AA-	
A1	A+	Upper
A2	A	Medium
A3	A-	Grade
Baa1	BBB+	Lower
Baa2	BBB	Medium
Baa3	BBB-	Grade
Ba1	BB+	Non
Ba2	BB	Investment
Ba3	BB-	Grade
B1	B+	Highly
B2	B	Speculative
B3	B-	
Caa1	CCC+	Substantial Risk
Caa2	CCC	Extremely Speculative
Caa3	CCC-	In Default
Ca	CC	Little Recovery
	C	Default
D	D	

Source: Learn Bonds, Bond Credit Ratings Table[12]

---

12 LearnBonds – Bond and Finance News, Bond Credit Ratings Table, David Waring, 6/4/2012, http://learnbonds.com/6891/bond-credit-ratings-table/.

Liquidity Risk

"Liquidity risk" refers to how quickly you can convert your assets to cash. A number of investments are marketable but not liquid. Marketable assets, such as your home, car, and valuable art, can be sold, but not quickly. It would be difficult to try and sell your home in one day if you had to raise cash. CDs and treasuries are highly liquid and can be converted to cash at a price close to the current market price. The key to converting your assets to cash is to make sure it can be done at a price you expect.

A highly rated stock or bond may be liquid, but there will be some price movement. You may end up selling at a price higher or lower than what you anticipated. Selling your stock in a rising market may mean selling at a price you expected. In a falling market, the opposite may be true. Bonds will trade up or down with interest rates. Selling a bond when interest rates are falling should deliver a higher price. Rising rates may bring a lower price. I recommend you keep a portion of your assets in liquid investments in the event you need to get your hands on some cash.

As you see, there are many faces of risk. The best way to reduce your risks in these categories is to have a diversified portfolio covering numerous asset classes.

CHAPTER 7
ASSET ALLOCATION

> *Invest in seven ventures, yes, in eight;*
> *you do not know what disaster*
> *may come upon the land.*
> ECCLESIASTES 11:2

Asset allocation is a useful tool for generating income and protecting your nest egg while staying diversified. There are numerous asset classes to choose from. Asset allocation is often confused with diversification, but they are two separate items. Asset allocation refers to spreading your investments across different asset classes. The assets you can own are stocks, bonds, real estate, gold, or cash. These different assets will help to reduce your risk. Diversification, on the other hand, can take place in a single asset class. For example, if you own twenty different stocks in your account, you're diversified within your stock allocation. If you own one bond, you're concentrated within your bond allocation.

If you're near or in retirement, you should focus on diversification. Remember: you don't want to put all your eggs in one basket.

An asset allocation strategy is like a Swiss Army Knife®. Swiss Army Knives come in all shapes and sizes. Some knives are simple with only a few tools to choose from; other knives have several options and are big and bulky. I own a few Swiss Army Knives and love them all. I bought one in Switzerland; it's huge with a ton of options. The Swiss Army Knife gives me choices, allowing me to use certain tools at certain times.

An account with diffcrent asset classes will give you choices, too. You'll use some asset classes more than others, giving you a solid set of tools you can call upon when needed.

As you approach retirement, it's important to focus on your investment allocation. It will determine your risk exposure and portfolio return.

There are many ways to approach asset allocation. A popular formula is to subtract your age from one hundred to determine your equity exposure.[13] If you're forty, you should have 60 percent of your money in stocks and 40 percent in bonds. If you're ninety, your stock exposure is 10 percent and bond exposure will be 90 percent. I'm not a fan of this formula because it doesn't take into consideration your current financial situation. I prefer to focus on how much money you'll need to achieve your financial goal.

---

13 *Is '100 Minus Your Age' Outdated?* Daniel Kurt, updated 11/20/2014, http://www.investopedia.com/articles/investing/062714/100-minus-your-age-outdated.asp.

If your goal is to retire with $1 million and your current investments are worth $1,500,000, you don't need much stock exposure. If you're ahead of your financial goal, you're in a position to get more conservative with your investments and preserve your wealth. On the flip side, if your current asset total is $500,000 and your goal is to retire with $1 million, you'll need more stock exposure for long-term growth.

Your comfort level for risk will also determine how much money you should allocate to stocks. Some people like roller coasters; others do not. Some people like volatility; others do not. You may be comfortable with 100 percent stock exposure while your next-door neighbor is better suited to owning all bonds.

One asset class you won't find in an income portfolio is commodities. Gold and other commodity investments are decent hedges for inflation or declining stock values, but they don't generate income. You may want to own them in your account for diversification purposes, however. Commodities are often referred to as an "alternative investment class" and may play an important part in your overall asset allocation. The suggested allocation to alternative or commodity investments is 5–10 percent of your portfolio.

Asset allocation doesn't prevent you from losing money. Just because your holdings are in different asset classes doesn't mean your investments won't lose value. In rising markets, a portfolio of 100 percent stocks will outperform an account invested in 100 percent bonds. When the stock market is falling, a 100 percent stock portfolio will lose a lot more than an account owning all bonds.

It's important to know all investments you can own will fall into three broad categories—safety, income, or growth. Investments will fall into one of these three buckets, and some will have their feet in more than one. The amount of money you have in each category will determine your risk and return. In retirement you'll need the three buckets to achieve your financial dreams. The stocks will be needed for long-term growth and income, bonds are added for income and safety, and cash is needed for income and liquidity. These three asset classes will work as a team to help you meet your financial goals.

The choices for asset allocation and diversification are numerous. Diversifying your holdings across asset classes has never been easier. The investments and account types are plentiful. A common stock can be held inside a mutual fund, exchange-traded fund, closed-end fund, unit investment trust, an annuity, or individually. This is the same for fixed-income investments.

A quick word about market timing: it can't be done. I'm often asked when the market will crash. I wish I knew—believe me! I'd love to buy at the bottom and sell at the top on a regular basis. If you own investments long enough, you will experience both strong- and weak-market cycles.

A 1986 study by Brinson, Hood, and Beebower found that the asset-allocation model accounted for 93.6 percent of returns.[14] The other 6.4 percent was attributed to security selection and market timing.

---

14 *The global case for strategic asset allocation.* Vanguard research, July 2012, https://personal.vanguard.com/pdf/s324.pdf.

The asset-allocation model allows you to become a better buy-and-hold investor. With a properly allocated portfolio, you're more likely to stay the course during tough times. It also pays to stay invested. According to Index Fund Advisors and the 2015 Dalbar QAIB Study the Standard & Poor 500 returned 11.06 percent from January 1, 1985, to December 31, 2014. How did the individual investor do during this bull run? The individual investor made 3.79 percent during this same time frame for a difference of 7.27 percent! To put this in dollar terms, if you didn't try to time the market but had gone along for the ride, you would have made an extra $2,021,388 (original investment of $100,000 on January 1, 1985, and held through December 31, 2014).

A better way to keep tabs on your investments is through your allocation. Your allocations to stocks, bonds, and cash are much easier to track than trying to time the markets. If you own 50 percent stocks and 50 percent bonds, you can easily follow your holdings and not worry about timing the market.

Let's fast-forward to the end of a year in which the stock market has done well. During your annual review with your advisor, you notice your stock allocation is now 70 percent and your bond allocation is 30 percent. In this model, it's easy to see your equity exposure is too high and your bond allocation is too low. In this situation you'd sell 20 percent of your stocks and transfer the cash to your bonds, making your allocation is once again back to 50 percent stocks and 50 percent bonds.

Rebalancing does not necessarily increase your returns, but it does help reduce risk over time. This is not market timing, but it can help you identify periods when some of your asset classes are more expensive than others.

Sometimes the best strategy is to sit and do nothing. Your patience will be rewarded over time. Doing nothing will also help keep your trading costs low and your taxes down. A magnolia tree can reach heights of eighty feet or more, but it needs a long time to reach its goal. You can't plant a magnolia tree today and dig it up tomorrow to check on the roots.

> *Someone is sitting in the shade today because someone planted a tree a long time ago.*
> —Warren Buffett

CHAPTER 8
DEBT

The borrower is slave to the lender.
—PROVERBS 22:7

Investors are always in search of their retirement number. I'm often asked, "What's my retirement number?" The retirement number, as we've already explored, is a combination of a multitude of inputs. One easy-to-calculate number is your debt level. Your debt number in retirement should be zero! It's important to try to eliminate all your debt. If you're debt-free, you'll have more options than those who are saddled with debt.

Unfortunately, the trend for retirees is to carry debt into their retirement years. According to the Consumer Financial Protection Bureau, the percentage of individuals ages seventy-five and older who carry a mortgage debt has increased from 8.4 percent in 2001 to 21.2

percent in 2011.[15] I doubt this trend will reverse course any time soon.

An argument I hear from investors is they do not want to forfeit the mortgage deduction. Can you find something better to spend your money on other than your mortgage payment? I could. The benefits of not having debt far outweigh your mortgage tax deduction. If you're worried about losing this tax deduction, I say give more money to your local church or charity. You'll not only get a tax deduction; you'll also be doing some much needed good.

---

15 *Mortgage debt – the new retirement time bomb.* Rodney Brooks, Washington Post 9/6/2015, https://www.washingtonpost.com/business/get-there/mortgage-debt–the-new-retirement-time-bomb/2015/09/04/eba628c6-500b-11e5-8c19-0b6825aa4a3a_story.html.

CHAPTER 9

Estate Planning for Income

> *I have seen something else under the sun:
> The race is not to the swift or the battle to
> the strong, nor does food come to the wise or
> wealth to the brilliant or favor to the learned;
> but time and chance happen to them all.*
> —*Ecclesiastes 9:11*

A home, for most families, is the largest asset in their estate. Your home is a nice place to live, but it's not the best investment to generate retirement income. In retirement your home may be more of a liability than an asset—especially if you have to replace a roof, upgrade an air-conditioning unit, or fix a pool pump.

Your estate can be used to generate income, provide you with tax benefits, and help others all at the same time. What's in your estate? Your estate is everything you own—stocks, bonds, real estate, cars, life insurance, and so forth.[16] The process of transferring your estate to your loved ones after you die is called estate planning. The items in your estate can transfer to the next generation by will, trust, beneficiary designation, title, or gift.

Is there an investment in your estate today that can benefit others? The ideal asset for transfer is one with a low-cost basis that doesn't generate income. Your basis refers to the price you paid to purchase your investment. If you purchased your investment at a low price, it has a low cost basis. The transfer of an investment with a low-cost basis into an estate-planning instrument will allow you to generate income, avoid capital-gains tax, and lower your taxable estate.

Another candidate for transfer is an asset with a heavy concentration. A concentration is a single asset controlling more than 25 percent of your total assets.[17] This concentration applies, more often than not, to publicly traded common stock.

Transferring your asset into an estate-planning vehicle will allow you to help others, such as nonprofit organizations. In addition, estate planning allows you to control who receives the money.

There are a number of estate-planning techniques you can employ to reduce your estate, but for our

---

[16] *What is My Estate?* The Greening Law Firm, P.C., http://www.greeninglawfirm.com/what-is-my-estate.htm.

[17] *Solutions for Concentrated Positions.* Steven Merkel, CFP, ChFC, Updated 1/30/2014, http://www.investopedia.com/articles/pf/05/concentratedstock.asp.

purposes I'll focus on two ideas to reduce your estate and generate income. The main goal for reducing your estate is to avoid paying an estate tax when you die. The current estate exclusion amount is $5.45 million per person and the maximum estate tax is 40 percent.[18] For example, if your estate is worth $10 million when you die you may own the IRS 40 percent of your estate or $1.82 million.

The first suggestion is a charitable remainder trust, or CRT.[19] Transferring assets to a CRT allows you to receive a tax deduction, lower your taxable estate, and receive income. The asset you transfer to the trust, whether a low-basis investment, land, or a concentrated holding, can be sold inside the trust, so you'll not incur any capital gains. The assets in the CRT can remain for a period certain not to exceed twenty years. A period certain can be five, ten or fifteen years. After the period is over your assets will revert to the designated charity and your income from the trust will cease. The deduction you receive will be the fair-market value of the asset minus the expected income at the time of the transfer to the CRT.

The income payments from the CRT will usually fall in a range of 5–8 percent. The income you receive from the trust will be taxable income. At your death or the

---

18 Certified Financial Planner Board of Standards, Inc. 2016 Estate and Gift Tax Rates and Exemptions, Appendix G: Provided Tax Tables.
19 *The Charitable Remainder Trust: Do Good and Get Tax Breaks.* Dennis Clifford, http://www.nolo.com/legal-encyclopedia/charitable-trust-tax-deduction-break-29702.html.

end of the term, your designated charity will receive the remainder of your assets.[20]

Let's explore an asset transfer into your new CRT. After much thought and planning, you decide to donate $1 million to your favorite charity. The asset you have chosen is a highly concentrated stock position you purchased many years ago that doesn't generate any income for you or your family. Your concentrated position cost you $250,000, and it's now worth $1 million. If you sold the stock in a taxable account, you'd pay a capital-gains tax on the $750,000 gain. By transferring the asset into the CRT, you can liquidate your investment inside the trust to avoid the capital-gains tax, diversify your holdings, receive monthly income, and get a charitable tax deduction. After you sell your stock, the CRT will be credited with $1 million (before selling expenses) in cash. The cash can now be invested in income generating assets. The $1 million in your CRT will pay you 5 percent, or $50,000, for the remainder of your life or term, not to exceed twenty years. Let's assume your CRT generated a 6 percent average annual return, and you live for another fifteen years. During this fifteen-year time frame, you receive $750,000 in income, and at the end of the term, your favorite charity will receive $1,232,759. In addition to your tax deduction and new income stream, you've lowered your taxable estate by over $1 million.

Your CRT can be structured as an annuity trust, unitrust, or pooled-income fund. The annuity trust will pay

---

[20] Constance J. Fontaine, *The Fundamentals of Estate Planning*, seventh edition, 406–409.

you a fixed amount, or an annuity, for the term of the trust. The annuity amount is fixed and does not change with the value of the portfolio.

The unitrust will pay a fixed percentage of the asset. This will benefit you if the asset in your CRT is rising, because it will generate more income as a result of the appreciated asset.

The pooled-income fund is similar to a mutual fund because your assets are comingled with other individuals inside the CRT.

Do you love your alma mater? Do you own real estate or other assets not generating income? If so, a private annuity may be your ticket. With a private annuity, you donate your asset to your alma mater, charity, or family member, and the recipient establishes a private annuity, providing you with a check for life.[21] The income from the annuity can be sent to you monthly, quarterly or annually. The income you receive is a function of the asset amount, your life expectancy, and the IRS section 7520 interest rate. The current IRS section 7520 rate is 1.8 percent.[22] The income must start prior to age 70.5. The private annuity allows you to transfer an asset with a low-cost basis or low yield to your alma mater and avoid a capital-gains tax. The institution or family member will sell the holding and establish your private annuity. The income you receive is part return from principal and part capital

---

21 Investopedia Private Annuity Definition, http://www.investopedia.com/terms/p/privateannuity.asp?o=40186&l=dir&qsrc=999&qo=investopediaSiteSearch.
22 IRS Section 7520 Interest Rates June 2016, https://www.irs.gov/Businesses/Small-Businesses-&-Self-Employed/Section-7520-Interest-Rates

gain. Once your basis has been absorbed, then your income is taxed as ordinary income.[23]

Let's look at an example. You own $1 million in raw land you'd like to donate to your alma mater. This is a tract of land you purchased for $100,000. Your alma mater will receive your land and then establish a private annuity for your benefit. Your donation will allow the university to use the $1 million. You'll receive the benefit of a charitable deduction, a lower taxable estate, and lifetime income. As in the example above, you live for fifteen more years. The income you will receive from this private annuity will be approximately $76,665, which is derived from your $1 million donation, the section 7520 interest rate, and your life expectancy.

A common question investors ask about donating money to an irrevocable estate vehicle is what to do about family members who won't receive the asset. When you transfer an asset to an irrevocable trust, the asset is removed from your estate and won't be received by your beneficiaries at your death. One option is to purchase life insurance in the amount of the gift you're donating. The life insurance should be purchased inside a life-insurance trust so that the death-benefit proceeds won't be included in your estate when you die. If you donated $1 million to a charitable remainder trust, you'd purchase a $1 million insurance policy to be paid out to your beneficiaries upon your death. The advantage of this strategy is you're able to benefit both your charity and your loved

---

[23] *Saving Money with a Private Annuity Trust*, George D. Lambert, http://www.investopedia.com/articles/retirement/06/privateannuity.asp.

ones. The main drawback is the cost of the life insurance as you age. The older you are, the higher the cost is to purchase life insurance.

These ideas can be win-win strategies for you and the organizations you love. Most estate-planning strategies are irrevocable, so make sure you do your homework before you move your assets. These two estate income-generation ideas are also easy to implement and administer.

CHAPTER 10
SYSTEMATIC WITHDRAWAL PLAN

*The plans of the diligent lead to profit
as surely as haste leads to poverty.*
—PROVERBS 21:5

How can you take advantage of the long-term trend of the stock market to generate income from your accounts? This leads us to the next strategy: the systematic-withdrawal plan. Here you withdraw a fixed dollar amount or fixed percentage from your mutual fund on a monthly basis. Once sold, you'll receive a monthly check. This strategy is the opposite of dollar-cost averaging, where you invest a constant dollar amount every month. The systematic-withdrawal plan is a way to turn your equity mutual fund into an income-producing asset.

Let's say you have accumulated $100,000 in XYZ mutual fund. With your $100,000 fund, you decide to withdraw 5 percent on an annual basis. This will generate $5,000 per year, or $416 per month. If your fund is growing at 8 percent per year and you're taking out 5 percent, you'll still have 3 percent net growth on your principal. Make sense?

Here is the math. You start with $100,000 and take out $416 per month. At the end of the calendar year, your mutual fund is now worth $103,126. If you continue with this strategy for ten years, you'd receive $49,920 in payments, and your original $100,000 mutual-fund investment would now be worth $145,000—not too shabby.

In this example, you set the 5 percent distribution at a constant rate. You can also use this strategy with a floating 5 percent distribution rate based on the year-end value of your mutual fund. If you end up with $110,000, you'd get a raise to $458 from $416. If it drops to $90,000, your income would drop to $375 per month. The systematic-withdrawal strategy will distribute income, dividends, capital gains, and principal to meet your monthly income needs.

The key for this strategy to work is to find the right balance of income you'd like to receive from your mutual fund. If you are withdrawing less than the account is earning, you'll never run out of money. The opposite is also true. If you're taking out more than the account is earning, it may run out of money.

Let's take a look at three solid mutual funds as examples for applying the systematic-withdrawal strategy. These three funds have stood the test of time and continue to be excellent candidates for a solid portfolio. In these examples you start with an investment of $100,000 and withdrawal 5 percent of the account balance every year.

The first fund is the Vanguard Standard & Poor 500 Index Fund (VFINX). This fund has been around since August 31, 1976. If you contributed $100,000 to this fund on January 1, 1985, your balance has risen to $459,551 on December 31, 2015. Your income from your original investment was $5,000 ($100,000 × .05). Applying a 5 percent systematic-withdrawal rate to this fund, you received $375,633 in total income during this thirty-year run! The current income for the coming year would be $22,977.55 ($459,551 × .05), which is a far cry from the original $5,000 you started off with in 1985.[24]

The next fund is Fidelity Magellan fund (FMAGX). The Magellan fund was established on May 2, 1963. This fund was made famous by the legendary fund manager Peter Lynch. Applying the same metrics to this fund as you did the Vanguard 500 fund, you have the following results: the original investment of $100,000 is now worth $463,408, and the annual income generated over the past thirty years was $450,993.[25]

The last fund is Investment Company of America (AIVSX). This fund was launched on January 1, 1934. The annual income generated from this strategy over the past thirty years was $412,737, and your December 31, 2015, value is $505,326. These are pretty impressive numbers from your original $100,000 investment.[26]

---
24 Morningstar Office® Online Tools Hypothetical Illustration.
25 Ibid.
26 Ibid.

These three funds, and many more, allowed you to take out 5 percent of your account value each year while continuing to grow the assets for future use. This is one of the best income strategies you can employ—especially in this low-interest-rate environment.

The systematic-withdrawal plan is a total return strategy using all the resources of your mutual fund.

CHAPTER 11

REQUIRED MINIMUM DISTRIBUTION

*So give back to Caesar what is Caesar's,
and to God what is God's.*
—MATTHEW 22:21

The required minimum distribution (RMD) isn't an income strategy per se, but you can manage your RMD to better help with your budgeting and cash flow during your retirement. At age 70.5 you have to remove a portion of your IRA as mandated by the IRS. This is called a required minimum distribution, and you must start to draw on your account by April 1 of the year after the year you turn 70.5.[27] The RMD is designed for you to withdraw the money from your account over your life expectancy.

---

[27] https://www.irs.gov/Retirement-Plans/Retirement-Plans-FAQs-regarding-Required-Minimum-Distributions.

The amount of money you're required to remove from your IRA is a function of the value of your IRA at the end of the previous year divided by a divisor set forth by the IRS life-expectancy tables. The math is simple. Let's say your previous year-end account value was $1 million, and the IRS divider is 20. When you divide your $1 million by 20, you get $50,000. This means you have to withdraw a minimum of $50,000 from your IRA. This process has to be repeated every year. You can take this distribution at any time between January 1 and December 31 of the current calendar year. The IRS doesn't care when you take the money out of your IRA, as long as you remove the money from your IRA during the calendar year.

The IRS treats all of your IRAs as one, so you can remove your RMD from one or all of your retirement accounts. Let's say you have ten IRA accounts totaling $1 million. The total balance of your IRAs is what is used to calculate your RMD.

What if you don't take out your required minimum distribution? The amount of your failed-distribution penalty is 50 percent of the amount you didn't remove. You would have to pay a $25,000 tax penalty on your $50,000 RMD. If you removed $40,000 from your IRA, then your penalty would be $5,000 or 50 per cent of $10,000 ($50,000 - $40,000 = $10,000). The 50 percent penalty only applies to the amount of money you were supposed to remove but didn't.

If you take your distribution on a monthly basis, this may help with your budgeting and cash-flow needs. In the above example, you need to remove $50,000 from your IRA at some point during the year. If you chose the monthly option, you can receive $4,166.67 per month.

Your distribution can be sent to you on a gross or net basis. If you decide to receive a net check, your IRA custodian can withhold the taxes due from your distribution. At the end of the year, you'll receive a 1099-R showing the amount of income received and the taxes paid to the IRS. The monthly income can be sent directly to your bank or brokerage account.

Another option is to remove the entire amount in January. Instead of receiving $50,000 over the course of twelve months, you'll receive the entire amount in the first month of the year, and you can use the money as you see fit. Again, this money can be sent to you as a gross or net check. In either case, the end result will be the same.

I prefer the monthly option solely for the benefit of helping with cash flow and budget planning.

CHAPTER 12
INTEREST RATES

He does not lend to them at interest or take a profit from them. He withholds his hand from doing wrong and judges fairly between two parties.
—EZEKIEL 18:8

The level of interest rates is a hot topic for investors, who always want to know if and when rates are rising or falling. Should you be concerned with the level of interest rates? Yes. Interest rates determine much about how you conduct your everyday living. When interest rates are low, it benefits the consumer. Everyone who buys goods and services will welcome low interest rates. With low interest rates, it's easier for individuals to purchase a home or a car. It also allows the business owner to expand into new areas.

But lower rates also have a dark side. They may give the soon-to-be homeowner or car buyer a false sense of wealth and encourage him or her to spend more than he or she can afford. Lower rates are also challenging to the retiree who's trying to generate income.

The lower the interest rate, the more assets you need to generate a desired level of income. If interest rates are 10 percent, you need $1 million to generate a $100,000 in annual income. At 2 percent, you need $5 million to generate this same level of income.

High interest rates are a boon for individuals living on a fixed income. A high-interest-rate environment allows you to generate more income with fewer assets. On the flip side, high interest rates are the bane of consumers—especially if you're trying to buy a big-ticket item like a home.

When interest rates are high, a homeowner might not be able to buy the home of his or her dreams. In 1985 the fixed rate for a thirty-year mortgage was 12.5 percent.[28] If you were going to purchase a home for $500,000 with a 20 percent down payment, your monthly payment on a mortgage of $400,000 would've been $4,269. Today, according to the website Bankrate®, the rate for a thirty-year mortgage is 3.84 percent. With the lower rate applied to your $500,000 home, the mortgage payment would be $1,872—a savings of $2,397 per month or $28,764 per year.

I know a number of people who have kept their money in checking or savings accounts, waiting for rates to rise. These individuals are reluctant to move their money

---

28 Mortgage rates history: 1985-2013, Denise Mazzucco, http://www.bankrate.com/finance/mortgage-rates-history-0112.aspx.

into longer-term investments for fear they'll miss a rise in rates. Interest rates have been falling steadily since the early 1980s. Will rates rise again? Of course. In the meantime, it's not wise to bury your money in these low-yielding vessels.

What's an income investor to do? How can you invest and not worry about the level of interest rates? In the chapters to follow, we'll explore a few strategies you can employ to help you generate more income on your money while not worrying about the level of interest rates.

CHAPTER 13

FUNDS

Victory is won through many advisers.
—PROVERBS *11:14*

Exchange-traded funds (ETFs) are one of the newer additions to the investment scene.[29] The ETF market has exploded as investors increasingly look for economical and efficient ways to invest in the market—all markets. An ETF will trade like a stock so you can place your order at any time during the trading day. This is a huge advantage for individuals wanting to trade intraday.

Even though an ETF trades like a stock, it's also similar to a traditional mutual find. Like a mutual fund, it will include a number of securities for a specific purpose. It will also have a prospectus detailing the structure of the fund, including the manager, fees, holdings, and so forth. An ETF will own investments in an index like the

---

29 Investopedia definition Exchange-Traded Fund (ETF), http://www.investopedia.com/terms/e/etf.asp.

S&P 500, the Dow Jones, or any of the numerous indices available.

You can purchase ETFs for specific sectors such as technology, health care, energy, or financials. If you're not sure if you should buy stock in Pepsi, Coke, or Dr. Pepper, you can buy them all in one package through an ETF.

ETFs are passive investments without a portfolio manager actively managing the investments and trying to determine which stock to buy or sell. The role of a portfolio manager for an ETF is to make sure the investments are in line with the underlying index. The ETF will own all or most of the investments held in a particular index. You can actively manage a passive portfolio by buying and selling throughout the trading day. I wouldn't recommend this strategy, but you do have the option of pursuing an active management style with passive-index ETFs.

How large is the ETF market? According to the Investment Company Institute®, the net assets in the ETF market at the end of 2014 were $1.974 trillion.[30] This, according to ICI, is about 13 percent of the net assets managed by mutual funds.

Traditional mutual funds are portfolios of individual investments—stocks, bonds, commodities, and so on.[31] They can be either actively or passively managed. In an active mutual fund, a portfolio manager or team of

---

30 Investment Company Institute ®, FAQ's about the U.S. ETF Market, https://www.ici.org/pubs/faqs/faqs_etfs_market.
31 Investopedia definition What is a 'Mutual Fund,'http://www.investopedia.com/terms/m/mutualfund.asp.

portfolio managers will try to time and beat the market with their investment research and selections.

Mutual funds are considered open ended, meaning they constantly issue new shares. This structure will keep the value of the fund from trading at a premium or discount to the underlying assets. A fund will trade at a premium if the current value of the fund is worth more than the assets in the fund. For example, if a fund is trading for $10 and the underlying assets are worth $8, then it's trading at a $2 premium. The premium or discount is usually found in a closed end fund which we will discuss shortly.

Mutual funds are probably the most recognized investment because they are widely held in 401(k)s, IRAs, and brokerage accounts. Actively managed mutual funds have increased competition as a result of the rise in index funds. With an index fund, you are buying a basket of stocks or bonds from a set index such as the Standard & Poor's 500 stock index. The advantages of buying an index fund are lower fees than an actively managed fund and lack of style drift.

Style drift occurs when a large stock, such as Apple (AAPL), starts to appear in not only large-cap mutual funds but also small-cap, international, or emerging-market funds. The prospectus of an actively managed mutual fund is written in broad terms so that the fund manager has the ability to buy nearly any investment she sees fit for the fund. If you own four or five actively managed stock mutual funds, you might have a position for Apple in each fund. Style drift could put you in a position of owning too much of one stock.

Mutual funds price at the end of the trading day meaning the buys and sells will be added up for the day and issue a closing price for the fund. The closing price you see at the end of the trading day is what is meant by "price" at the end of the day. If you buy a mutual fund at 9:30 a.m. EST, the fund will not price until the end of the day, after the market closes at 4:00 p.m. EST. This may be an issue. For example, you want to sell your mutual fund on a day when the stock market is doing well. After you place your order in the morning, you leave for work and don't check your order again until you return home. At some point during the day, the stock market reversed course and closed substantially down. Your sell order was executed at the close of the day and not when you placed the order, causing a significant difference in price. This is something to beware of when you are buying or selling mutual funds. I recommend placing your buy or sell order later in the afternoon so you have a better understanding of what your fund may do at the end of the day. For example, if the stock market is up 200 points at 2:00 EST, this would be a good day to sell your mutual fund.

The closed-end fund (CEF) is an outlier investment few investors have added to their portfolio.[32] The closed-end fund was popular until exchange-traded funds made their entrance on the main stage. CEFs are similar to mutual funds (open-end) and exchange-traded funds

---

[32] Investopedia definition Closed-End Fund, http://www.investopedia.com/terms/c/closed-endinvestment.asp.

in that they hold a number of individual investments for a particular type of investment, such as corporate or tax-free bonds. Closed-end funds are publicly traded investments. Holdings inside the fund will dictate your level of income and investment return. Similar to other types of packaged products, a closed-end fund can own stocks, bonds, and other asset classes.

The main difference between a closed-end bond fund and a traditional mutual fund is that a closed-end fund will issue a fixed number of shares—thus the term "closed." This fixed-share issue will result in your closed-end fund trading at a discount or a premium to its net asset value (NAV). The premium and discount is a function of the current price of the fund relative to the underlying assets in the fund. A fund trading at $10 owning assets worth $15 is trading at a $5 discount. This can create opportunities to purchase these investments at a discount to their underlying assets while at the same time generating a nice level of monthly income. Ideally, you want to buy a closed-end fund when it's trading at a discount so that when—or if—it trades at a premium you can sell it and lock in your profit.

As with any investment, valuation matters. I'd caution against buying a closed-end fund when it's trading at a substantial premium to the underlying asset. It doesn't make sense to buy an investment for $15 when it's underlying assets are worth $10. I'd also avoid a fund carrying too much leverage. The leverage in a closed-end fund is how the fund manager can generate above-average income.

The yield on these investments can be over 5 percent, with a number approaching the 10 percent level. It's possible to find a closed-end fund for most asset classes and bond types. For example, an investor who wants to receive tax-free income from a portfolio of California tax-free bonds will be able to choose from a number of state-specific closed-end bond fund offerings.

Where can you find information on funds? The best way is to buy a copy of *Barron's* magazine on Saturday morning and search the stock and fund tables. *Barron's* will have a section devoted to all funds—ETFs, traditional mutual funds, and closed-end funds. The fund listings will highlight category, name, objective, premium or discount, yield, returns, and much more. It's a helpful resource to use for fund research. Once you have the symbol of the fund you want to own, you can do additional research at Yahoo! Finance or Morningstar. These online resources will have the ability to screen for fund holdings as well.

Funds come in all shapes and sizes—ETF, traditional and closed end. The three types of funds can own the same underlying assets, so pick the style that best fits your investment needs.

CHAPTER 14
Bond Definitions

*You will be secure, because there is hope;
you will look about you and
take your rest in safety.*
—JOB 11:18

Fixed-income investments—or bonds, as they are often called—come in a multitude of flavors, from guaranteed US Treasuries to high-yielding corporate junk bonds. They have the following characteristics: a coupon, issue date, issue price, call feature, and maturity date. Bonds and other fixed-income investments are issued with a prospectus so you'll be able to review all the terms of your new investment.

The coupon is the fixed component of your bond and is where we get the term "fixed income." When you buy a bond with a coupon, the coupon rate will not change for as long as you own the bond. For example, if you purchase a thirty-year tax-free bond paying 5 percent interest, you'll receive 5 percent per year regardless of what is happening to current interest rates or the price of your bond.

The bond will be issued at a certain price—usually $100. The price of $100 is considered par. When you hear the term "discount" or "premium" in the bond world, it's the function of the current price of the bond relative to the par value. A bond selling for $105 is trading at a $5 premium to the par value of $100, while a bond priced at $95 is trading at a $5 discount to the par value of $100. What causes the discount or premium? Interest rates. If interest rates fall, the price of your bond will rise.

Let's look at a 5 percent fixed-coupon bond. The coupon is fixed, so if interest rates drop to 4 percent, your bond is now more valuable because it was issued at 5 percent. As a result, the value of your bond will rise. The coupon is fixed, but the price is not. A bond with a 5 percent coupon maturing in thirty years purchased at $100 will rise to $117.29 if rates drop to 4 percent.

The call feature on the bond will give the issuer of your bond the option to redeem the bond before maturity. It'll give the issuer an exit if he or she issues a bond with a high interest rate and rates start to fall. It's usually set for ten years from the issue date. Bonds issued in the late 1970s and early 1980s had high coupons, so when interest rates started to fall, the bonds with call features were being redeemed. A bond issuer without a call feature had to pay the high interest rate until the bond matured. Bonds issued by the US government—such as bills, notes, and bonds—do not have call features.

The maturity date on a bond is when it will mature and return your principal to you. This is one of the main differences between owning an individual bond and a bond fund. With an individual bond, you know at some point your bond will mature and your principal will be returned to your account. This maturity date can last from a few days to a few decades, so despite what the investment landscape looks like during the life of your bond, you can rest easy knowing at some point it will mature.

A bond fund does not have this luxury. It has an infinite life and can go on forever. This may be a challenge when interest rates are rising, because when rates rise, prices fall. I like to use the analogy of swimming in a pool versus swimming in the ocean. An individual bond, like a swimming pool, has defined borders, and if needed, you can grab the side of the pool for safety and climb out. If you're swimming in the middle of the ocean, trying to reach safety could be a challenge.

The current yield on a bond will fluctuate based on the coupon payment and the price of the bond. The current yield is a way for you to compare similar types of investments. A bond with a 5 percent coupon trading at par will have the same current yield of 5 percent (5% / $100 = 5%). One trading at $95 and paying a 5 percent coupon rate will have a current yield of 5.26 percent (5% / $95 = 5.26%). A bond paying 5 percent with a price of $105 will have a current yield of 4.76 percent (5% / $105 = 4.76%). Again, the coupon is fixed; everything else will fluctuate like the current yield.

UP THE INCOME LADDER

The yield to maturity will also move with the price of the bond. However, the day you purchase your bond the coupon, the current yield and yield to maturity are locked in until it's redeemed by the issuer or until you sell it. The yield to maturity is another way to compare bonds with different coupons and prices. I call it the equalizer. It's what you will earn over the life of the bond once everything is said and done.

A 5 percent bond trading at par, or $100, will have the same coupon, current yield, and yield to maturity. A thirty-year bond with a 5 percent coupon trading at $95 will have a yield to maturity of 5.33 percent. Notice the yield to maturity is higher than both the current yield and the coupon payment. The same bond trading at $105 will have a yield to maturity of 4.68 percent, which is lower than both the coupon rate and current yield.

Let's explore a hypothetical bond issued by the City of Bondsville, USA. This bond was issued on January 1, 2010 with a coupon of 4 percent, an issue price of $100, and a maturity of January 1, 2020. The coupon, current yield, and yield to maturity are all the same, since the bond was issued at $100. This bond will pay interest every six months—January 1 and July 1. If you purchase ten bonds at $100, your purchase price will be $10,000, and your bonds will generate an annual income of $400. The income is paid every six months in the amount of $200. During the ten-year life of this bond, you'll receive $4,000 in interest payments ($400 × 10 years = $4,000), and at maturity you'll get back your initial investment of $10,000.

Let's say three years after you bought your bond, interest rates dropped to 3 percent. Your bond has seven years left until maturity, so the new price of the bond will be $106.23. The price of your bond is more valuable because rates dropped to 3 percent. Your bond is now trading at a premium to the original purchase price of $100.

If rates rise to 5 percent, the new price of your 4 percent bond will be $94.21. It's now trading at a discount or below $100, because rates have risen 1 percent. Why would an investor pay $100 for your bond paying 4 percent when they can buy a new bond paying 5 percent?

The price of this bond, and all bonds, will fluctuate with interest rates because the coupon is fixed. If interest rates rise, the price of the bond will fall. If interest rates fall, the price of the bond will rise. Remember the seesaw in the park?

Of course, the equalizer in all of this is the yield to maturity. If you recall, the yield to maturity is what you'll earn once everything is said and done. The yield to maturity includes the price you paid, the income you received, and the return of your principal. The yield to maturity will be highest for the bond purchased at a discount and lower for the one purchased at a premium. The yield to maturity is one way to compare bonds across years, sectors, and types.

A type of fixed-income investment helpful for income and planning goals is the zero-coupon bond. It can come in all types of bonds—corporate, municipal, and US Treasury. Zero-coupon bonds don't have a coupon, so there is no annual income you'll receive when you own these bonds. Since these bonds do not have a coupon, they are called "zero-coupon." They are purchased at a discount to the maturity value of $1,000. Even though this bond does not have a coupon payment, it is accruing interest at a stated rate, which determines the current price. These bonds will still be affected by a change in interest rates because they were issued with a fixed rate.

Why talk about a zero-coupon bond as a way to generate income in retirement? These bonds work well in a bond ladder in which bonds come due every year or so. They can also help fund a future liability, such as a tuition payment or car purchase. You'll be able to buy a future liability at a discount and use the remainder of the money for other investments. For example, if you purchase a zero-coupon bond with a thirty-year maturity, the price you might pay would be $350. You can buy it at $350 and it'll mature to $1,000 in thirty years. If you bought one hundred bonds, the total purchase price would be $35,000, and they would mature to $100,000. The extra $65,000 you'd have spent on a bond with a coupon can now be invested in another investment, such as a stock-index fund.

Now that you've had a primer on bonds, let's look at these investments to see how they might fit into your investment portfolio for generating income in retirement.

CHAPTER 15

THE BOND LADDER

Honest scales and balances belong to the Lord;
all the weights in the bag are of his making.
—PROVERBS 16:11

One of the best ways to protect yourself against rising or falling interest rates is to build a bond ladder—that is, a portfolio of bonds with different maturities.[33] Ladders come in all shapes and sizes.

The maturities are similar to rungs on a ladder, and each one you climb gets you closer to your goal. Your ladder can own bonds maturing in thirty days or thirty years. The ladder you construct should suit your specific situation and time frame. You can also own multiple ladders designed for different financial goals.

How do you construct a ladder? Let's look at an example. You can start by buying five bonds with maturities

---

33 Investopedia definition Bond Ladder, http://www.investopedia.com/terms/b/bondladder.asp

UP THE INCOME LADDER

ranging from one to five years, with corresponding rates of 1, 2, 3, 4, and 5 percent. The average yield will be 3 percent, and the average maturity will be 3 years. At the end of the first year, you'll receive a portion of your principal back from the maturing one-year bond. With the cash from this bond, you'll buy a new five-year bond paying 5 percent. The remaining bonds in your ladder have now moved up by one year. Your bond ladder now consists of bonds maturing in two, three, four, five, and five years, paying 2, 3, 4, 5, and 5 percent. The average yield of your bond ladder is now 3.8 percent, while the average maturity stays the same. The average maturity stays the same because you still own a portfolio of bonds coming due every year for five years.

At the end of the second year, bond number two is now due. With the proceeds from bond two, you purchase a five-year bond paying 5 percent. The remaining bonds now are one year closer to maturing. Your bond ladder now consists of bonds with maturities of three, four, five, five, and five years. It's now paying 3, 4, 5, 5, and 5 percent, with an average rate of 4.4 percent. This process can be repeated indefinitely.

A bond ladder will always have bonds maturing, so you get the benefit of liquidity while at the same time enjoying above-average income from your long-term bonds. The income from the original ladder was 3 percent, and by the last example it jumped to 4.4 percent—an increase of 46 percent. At the same time your average maturity stayed the same at 3 years. If interest rates start to rise, you'll have bonds coming due, allowing you to buy bonds with higher interest rates. If rates fall or stay the same, you have locked in a few longer-dated and higher-paying bonds.

The bond ladder is flexible, allowing you to use any type of fixed-income investment to construct your portfolio: CDs, tax-free municipal bonds, corporate bonds, or US Treasuries. You can mix and match with the fixed-income choices available to you and your portfolio. For example, you can construct a ladder with US Treasuries, corporate bonds, and tax-free municipal bonds. The treasuries can be short term—from one to two years—the corporate bonds from two to ten, and the municipal bonds from ten to thirty years.

Do you have to use individual investments for your ladder, or can it be built with mutual funds or exchange-traded funds? You certainly can use these funds to fund your ladder. When constructing a ladder using ETFs or mutual funds, make sure they have different objectives for the types of bonds they are allowed to own.

The funds you ultimately own should have exposure to short-, intermediate-, and long-term bonds. A portfolio of bond ETFs might consist of three ETFs: the IShares 1 to 3 Year Treasury Bond ETF (SHY), which owns government bonds maturing in one to three years; the IShares 10 to 20 Year Treasury Bond ETF (TLH), which owns bonds maturing in ten to twenty years; and finally, the IShares 20+ Year Treasury Bond ETF (TLT), with government bonds maturing beyond twenty years. A portfolio of SHY, TLH, and TLT would have a current yield of 1.73 percent. With an all-ETF ladder, you don't need to make any regular changes to your account, as the investments inside the ETFs will be managed by the fund company.

Even though you can use mutual funds or ETFs for your ladder, I recommend using individual bonds. A ladder works best when there are specific maturity dates attached to your portfolio.

As I mentioned, investors often have a high percentage of cash in their accounts waiting for interest rates to rise. What if you don't want to commit your cash or capital to a long-term investment strategy or a bond ladder owning long-term bonds? At the same time, you are not excited about keeping your money in a money-market fund earning .01 percent. What should you do? A typical money-market fund will own short-term investments like CDs and treasury bills. The advantage of a money-market fund is the daily liquidity at a price of one dollar per share.

A money-market fund is stable. However, if you don't need daily liquidity, you can use these same short-term investments to create your own money-market fund with better results. In exchange for the friendly confines of a money-market fund, you'll be able to pick up a higher rate for your cash. The other advantage of creating your own money market is that your investments will be guaranteed and insured. If you invest in CDs or US Treasury investments, your investments are either FDIC insured or an obligation of the US government. In the case of a short-term US treasury ladder, your insurance coverage is unlimited! This is not the case with a standard-issue money-market fund, as it is only insured to $250,000.

What would your personal money-market fund look like? It might consist of short-term CDs maturing every three months—at three, six, nine, and twelve months. In this short-term ladder, your money matures every three months, and your rate is higher than a typical money-market fund.

A number of years ago, I helped a client construct a short-term ladder. He called to ask how I invest a lot of money but was reluctant to tell me how much money he had to invest because he didn't have a lot invested through me at the time. He finally told me he'd inherited a few million dollars and was in the process of calling local banks to get their current CD rates. He wanted his newfound wealth insured. I informed him he'd have to invest his money with fifteen different banks to qualify for the full FDIC insurance coverage. We set up a short-term US Treasury Bill ladder guaranteed by the US government. I was able to offer him one-stop shopping while he settled the estate. This also gave us time to come up with a long-term investment plan for him and his family. It was through this short-term bond ladder we were able to create his own personal money-market fund.

In summary, a bond ladder built for you and your family can help you achieve your financial goals without worrying about interest rates rising or falling.

CHAPTER 16
INVESTMENTS

> *And God is able to bless you abundantly, so that in all things at all times, having all that you need, you will abound in every good work.*
> —2 CORINTHIANS 9:8

After your financial plan is complete and your asset allocation is determined, it's now time to invest. There are numerous investment choices, and they can be boiled down to three categories—growth, income, or safety. Stocks are for growth, bonds for income, and cash for safety. These investments can be purchased individually, in mutual or exchange-traded funds, and in a few other structures. I prefer to use individual investments and index funds to keep expenses low and transparent. With direct ownership of stocks and bonds, you get the benefit of the growth and income as it happens. For example, when Pepsi pays their quarterly dividend, it'll be credited to your account the same day. The same will happen with a Travis County municipal-bond interest payment. The interest a bond pays will be credited to your account when it pays. A mutual fund, on the other hand, will collect all the dividend and interest income and pay it to their shareholders quarterly or annually.

Direct ownership of individual securities and low-cost index funds is the most economical way to own investments. You can access a variety of investments through the purchase of these low-cost holdings. Two of the best fund families for index and low-cost investments are Dimensional Fund Advisors and the Vanguard Group.

Let's look at specific investments for your retirement portfolio. We'll start with conservative investments and work our way toward the aggressive ones. It's important to note that all investments, whether conservative or aggressive, have risks. The risks might not be apparent at first, but they exist in one form or another.

Our first investment stop will be cash.

CHAPTER 17
CASH

> *Be on your guard; stand firm in the*
> *faith; be courageous; be strong.*
> —1 CORINTHIANS *16:13*

What is cash? Does it mean $100 bills in your safe-deposit box? It could. However, for an investor, it probably means a savings account or money-market fund. These investments are safe, solid, and accessible.

Why should you incorporate cash into your investment plan? Does it make sense to add cash to your accounts as a way to increase your income? One of the key advantages of cash is that it doesn't go down in value and is immune to the short-term moves of the stock market. This vanilla-flavored investment allows your other investments to do their thing—which, in turn, allows you to generate more income.

Cash allows bonds to generate income and stocks to create wealth. It's also a safe haven when the world financial markets are not cooperating. With a solid cash foundation, you're more likely to hold your growth and income investments in a time of crises. It's also a direct beneficiary of a rising-interest-rate environment. When interest rates start to rise, you should see an increase in your income from the money you hold in cash accounts.

What's the right amount of cash to have on hand? According to Christine Benz of Morningstar, she'd recommend between six months' and two years' worth of expenses in cash.[34]

I recommend three years' worth of cash in a savings account or money-market fund as you approach retirement. If your expenses are $100,000 per year, your three-year cash number will be $300,000. This cash level will help cushion the blow of a declining stock market. It will also protect you in the event you retire during a stock-market correction.

Three years' worth of cash will allow you to continue spending without being forced to sell your investments at a low point. Your three-year cash cushion would have saved you a lot of heartache and sleepless nights if you retired in March of 2000 or October of 2007. You'd have been able to tap into your cash account while you waited for the stock market to recover. The cash you held in your accounts wouldn't have dropped during the Tech Wreck of 2000 or the Great Recession of 2008. It would

---

[34] http://socialize.morningstar.com/NewSocialize/utility/Article.ashx?TID=358844&AID=746669&SID=100001026&T=2.

have retained its value and allowed you to cover your living expenses. It would have also allowed your other investments to recover in value before you had to make any changes to your portfolio.

If you didn't hold cash during these troubling times, you may have been forced to sell stocks at a significant loss (30 percent, 50 percent, or more). Selling during a market meltdown will endanger your recovery potential and long-term investment returns. During the Tech Wreck of 2000, I was talking to a friend who was complaining about his portfolio losing value. I asked how much money he had invested in cash or bonds. He didn't own any bonds and held little cash. He was forced to sell stocks at disastrous prices in order to raise cash. Had he maintained a cash cushion, he could've ridden out the storm and let his growth investments come back to life. Cash is a tremendous resource for both emergencies and opportunities.

What if you're not ready to retire? With interest rates near zero for cash accounts, does it make any sense to hold a cash position? My answer is maybe. If you're retiring in five years or more and most of your money is in a company-sponsored retirement plan, you should hold little, if any, cash in this type of account. In your IRA account or taxable account, the level of cash you hold will be a function of how much risk you are willing to take. A more conservative investor may have 20–30 percent of his or her investments in cash, while a more aggressive investor might hold 5–10 percent.

I'm often asked by clients how they can generate more income from their cash. I always respond with the same question: "What if we move your money from cash into an investment that may lose value?"

The reply is usually as follows: "Oh, I can't lose any of this money." With this response it's best to keep your ultra-safe money in a cash account.

How much can you allocate to cash? In terms of an allocation, you can invest 100 percent of your portfolio in cash. A 100 percent allocation will give you short-term safety, but in the long term, you'll lose out on the growth of your capital. In addition to the lost opportunity to grow your money, your cash will lose value to inflation.

What if you have too much cash and you want to earn more income? Let's explore some alternatives to cash so you can earn more money on your savings. As I mentioned, we will work our way from conservative to aggressive investments. The next stop on our journey is the always-popular certificate of deposit.

CHAPTER 18

CERTIFICATES OF DEPOSITS

*Have I not commanded you? Be
strong and courageous.*
—JOSHUA 1:9

A certificate of deposit (CD) is often the first place savers turn to when they have too much cash in their checking, savings, or money-market account. CDs are a flexible investment. A CD can be tailored to fit into most portfolios and is a time deposit with maturities ranging from a few weeks to twenty years. However, most savers rarely venture far out from one maturing past three to six months. The short-term nature of a CD is comforting to people because they know in a few months, their principal will be returned. The interest rates on CDs are low relative to other types of fixed-income investments, such as corporate or municipal bonds, due to the FDIC coverage.

One advantage of a CD is the FDIC insurance coverage up to $250,000 per person, per bank, and per account.[35] For example, a husband and wife open the following accounts at their bank: two single accounts, a joint account, and two IRAs. They have five accounts at the bank, meaning they can insure up to $1,250,000 in bank CDs (5 × $250,000). This level of safety and insurance coverage is a big reason why so many savers trust their millions to their local brick-and-mortar bank.

When a CD matures beyond one year, it's possible you'll receive your income payments every six months. When it matures, you can use the proceeds for any purpose or reinvest your principal and interest into a new CD.

As I mentioned, most people will store up their savings in very short-term CDs. A reason for this is savers are waiting for interest rates to rise. They don't want to lock up their money in longer-term CDs for fear interest rates will rise and they'll lose out on the opportunity to reinvest at a higher rate. The three- and six-month CDs are huge beneficiaries of this rising-rate mentality.

How can a saver use CDs to generate more income in retirement? The first idea is to purchase CDs with longer maturities. A CD maturing in one, two, or five years will pay more interest than a three- or six-month CD. The longer-term CDs are insured and guaranteed as well.

---

[35] Federal Deposit Insurance Corporation, Understanding Deposit Insurance, https://www.fdic.gov/deposit/deposits/.

UP THE INCOME LADDER

Are you concerned about rising interest rates, or do you want to take advantage of a special rate promotion at your bank? If so, you can set up a CD ladder. Your ladder will allow you to take advantage of rising or falling interest rates.

Let's say you want to invest $250,000 in a CD. You don't need the money, but you can't risk losing it either. In this scenario you'll most likely invest your money into a three-month CD, wait until it matures, and then make another decision. This is a simple strategy and only takes a few minutes to set up. A ladder will increase your income and provide liquidity. In your ladder you can invest $50,000 in five different maturities—three months, six months, nine months, twelve months, and eighteen months. You'll have $50,000 coming due every three months while at the same time earning a higher rate of interest on your longer-dated CDs. Rates today can range from .25 percent on the short end to over 3.25 percent for CDs maturing beyond twenty years.

What if you invest in a longer-term CD and you need the money? The answer to this question depends on where you purchased the CD, because CDs are offered by both banks and brokerage firms. CDs issued by a bank won't show any fluctuation in value, whereas a CD purchased through a brokerage firm will fluctuate with interest rates similar to other types of bonds. If you bought your CD through a bank and you need the money, they will most likely penalize you for a few months of interest and then return your principal.

If you bought your CD through a brokerage firm, you may get back more or less than your original investment. The brokerage firm will not charge you a penalty, but your principal portion may be more or less than your original cost. Like other types of fixed-income investments, the price of your CD will rise or fall with interest rates.

If you're used to keeping large amounts of money in a checking, savings, or money-market account, I recommend moving the money to CDs so you can get a higher return on your cash. You can invest 100 percent of your assets into CDs. The short-term safety and long-term risks will be similar to cash, but CDs will give you a higher rate of return on your investment.

If you have been a long-term CD buyer, it may be time for you to invest in other types of fixed-income investments, such as treasury, corporate, or municipal bonds. These fixed-income investments may give your portfolio a new outlook and better returns.

CHAPTER 19

US TREASURIES

For you have been my refuge…
—PSALM *61:3*

The next stop on our tour is the US Treasury market. They're backed by the full faith and credit of the US government, a guarantee most investors crave. The backing by the government means the interest rate you will receive will be low when compared to other types of income investments without a guarantee. If it's safety you're looking for, you've found a friend in the US Treasury market.

The US Treasury market allows you to purchase bonds maturing anywhere from a few days to thirty years in the future. Treasury investments are issued as bills, notes, and bonds and can be purchased at TreasuryDirect or through your advisor.[36]

---

36 TreasuryDirect®, Treasury Securities & Programs, http://www.treasurydirect.gov/indiv/products/products.htm.

T-bills usually have a $10,000 minimum investment and are sold at a discount to their maturity value of par, or $1,000. If you buy a six-month T-bill priced at $99.67, your cost will be $9,967, and at maturity, you'll receive $10,000.

T-notes and T-bonds are sold in $1,000 increments and can trade above or below $1,000 depending on interest rates. Interest on these investments will be paid every six months. T-notes have maturities ranging from one to ten years, while T-bonds have maturities from ten to thirty years. The rates on US Treasuries currently yield .25 percent to 2.5 percent, depending on the maturity.

US Treasuries are an excellent source for income and safety. The interest is also free from state and local taxes, a big deal if you live in California or New York.

US Treasury investments also come in the form of zero-coupon bonds. Zeroes are excellent choices for IRAs, because you don't have to worry about paying income taxes on the interest.

A US Treasury zero-coupon bond can be used to pay for future events with discounted dollars, such as paying off your home mortgage. Let's say you decide to pay off your home in ten years and you determine you'll need $150,000 to make this happen. You can buy a US Treasury zero-coupon bond with a face value at maturity of $150,000 for $123,052 (ten years at a 2 percent yield). When it matures, you can use the $150,000 to pay off your mortgage.

Another popular Treasury investment is the TIP.[37] TIP stands for "treasury inflation-protected securities." TIPs

---

37 TreasuryDirect®, TIPS in Depth, http://www.treasurydirect.gov/indiv/research/indepth/tips/res_tips.htm.

allow you to benefit from a rise in inflation and to keep your purchasing power in line with the rate of inflation. An increase in inflation will increase the principal portion of your investment. They are issued with maturities of five, ten, and thirty years. The interest on a TIP will be paid every six months. TIPS can be purchased in secondary market on any day of the week.

The treasury market has a low correlation with stocks, meaning when stocks are falling, treasuries are rising and vice versa. According to Morningstar, the correlation of large-cap stocks to long-term government bonds was .01 from 1972 to 2014.[38] This low correlation makes it a good hedge for your stock portfolio.

You can watch this action on a daily basis. When there's good news in the world, the stock market will rise and the treasury market will fall as people sell safe assets to buy riskier assets. When people are concerned about a falling stock market, they buy US Treasuries. They'll sell stocks and buy bonds until there is an all-clear signal to come out of the shelter and venture back into the stock market.

This cycle repeats itself constantly. You can follow this action by using two exchange-traded funds to track stock and bond markets. The Vanguard S&P 500 Index ETF symbol is VOO, and the iShares 20+ Year Treasury Bond ETF symbol is TLT. These two ETFs will allow you to watch the stock- and bond-market dynamics in real time. On a strong up day in the stock market, VOO will trade

---

[38] *Market Results for Stocks, Bonds, Bills and Inflation 1926 – 2014.* Morningstar ® Ibbotson®SBBI® 2015 Classic Yearbook, page 56.

higher, while TLT will be lower. The price action of these two will reverse itself when the stock market is falling.

Don't overlook the guaranteed feature of US Treasury investments. As you recall, the FDIC insurance coverage for CDs is $250,000 per person, per account; with US Treasuries the guarantee is unlimited. If you buy a T-note for $1 million, your entire $1 million investment is guaranteed.

With the features and flexibility of the treasury market, it's possible to set up a number of investment strategies for your accounts. The most popular strategy for buying multiple bonds is the bond ladder. The US Treasury bond ladder can be constructed with any combination of bills, notes, or bonds. A bond ladder can be short term or stretch out to thirty years.

The barbell is another strategy you can employ with these bonds. If you've ever lifted weights, you know a barbell has weight on both ends and a bar in the middle. With a barbell strategy, you purchase short-term T-bills and long-term T-bonds. Let's say you have $100,000 to invest. You allocate $50,000 to a three-month T-bill and $50,000 to a thirty-year T-bond. Of course, you can create any length of barbell you wish. Using a barbell strategy will give you constant liquidity and the ability to lock in longer-term rates.

Another popular strategy is to match your future liability with the bond of your choice. For example, if you are going to retire in fifteen years, you can purchase a T-bond with a fifteen-year maturity date. The liability matching allows you to have money available for any event, whether it be education or retirement.

You can put 100 percent of your investment into treasuries, similar to CDs and cash. The 100 percent allocation to treasuries is the ultimate in safety. Again, short-term safety reduces long-term growth.

We have explored the safest of the safe investments – cash, CDs and US Treasuries. These investments are solid choices for investors looking for safety and some income. It's now to look at investments where you can generate growth and income. If you've been an investor in the safe category, it's now time to climb the ladder and start to earn more income from your investments.

CHAPTER 20

MUNICIPAL BONDS

*There he brought the hungry to live,
and they founded a city where they could settle.*
—PSALM 107:36

"We built this city, we built this city on rock 'n' roll, built this city on rock 'n' roll." You no doubt have heard this song by Jefferson Starship. You're now singing the song out loud and can't get it out of your head—sorry!

However, with all due respect to Jefferson Starship, most cities were built with tax-free municipal bonds. They're issued by local or state agencies to help build roads, dams, bridges, schools, and other public works. You've likely had the opportunity to vote on a bond referendum or two over the years. It's not uncommon to see a vote on a local ballot for highway improvements or the building of a new school.

UP THE INCOME LADDER

When you vote on these public-work bonds, you're allowing the local government to issue a bond to finance the project. The money to pay for these bonds comes from your wallet. These bonds will generate their income from the taxes you pay or the services you use.

Bonds with issuers having the ability to tax you and your neighbors to pay the interest are referred to as general-obligation bonds. The general-obligation bonds, or G-O bonds as they are called, are some of the safest tax-free bonds around.

An issuer of a bond generating income from a project is called a revenue bond. The revenue from the project will fund the payment and pay for the bonds. The revenue bonds you'll vote on can be for an airport, public works, hospitals, or toll roads.[39] A portion of the money collected from the projects will go to the debt service for the bonds.

As a result of the bonds being used for the public good, the interest you receive is tax-free. The tax-free incentive is there so you'll invest in these bonds and help the local authorities raise money for their projects—schools, roads, and so forth. A number of states may issue taxable bonds, but we'll only focus on the tax-free bonds. The interest is free from local, state, and federal taxes; this is referred to as triple tax-free.

Municipals are an excellent choice for people who earn a high level of income. The higher your taxable income, the higher the after-tax return on your investment.

---

[39] *What are Revenue Bonds?* Morningstar® Investing Classroom, course 209: Revenue Bonds, http://news.morningstar.com/classroom2/course.asp?docId=5394&page=2.

Municipal bonds pay income every six months. Municipal bonds have a rate range today of .25 percent in the short term to over 4 percent for the long term.

To find out if you're getting a competitive tax-free rate relative to other bonds, you'll need to find the taxable equivalent yield on your bond. For example, a San Diego general-obligation bond paying 4 percent tax-free interest equates to a 6 percent taxable bond. The approximate math is the coupon rate on the tax-free bond multiplied by 1.5. In this example, the 4 percent coupon times 1.5 equals 6 percent. I use 1.5 as a quick and dirty guide to find the taxable equivalent rate. The actual formula is the coupon divided by one minus your tax bracket. It will look like this: coupon divided by (1 - your tax bracket). If your tax bracket is 35 percent, the formula is 4 percent/ (1 - 0.35) = 6.15 percent. So if you can find a taxable bond paying 6 percent or better for the same time frame, it would be better to purchase the taxable bond over the tax-free bond.

If you live in a state with an income tax, you'll want to buy bonds issued by the state in which you live. If you live in California or New York, you want to own bonds issued by your home state. If you live in California and buy a bond issued in Florida, the income you receive will be taxable at the state level. If you live in a state with no state income tax, like Texas, you can buy bonds issued from any state.

Up to this point, we have talked about allocating 100 percent of your assets (if you wanted to) to cash, CDs, or US Treasuries. I recommend capping your allocation to

50 percent or 75 percent when buying municipal bonds. Tax-free bonds are popular investments, but they lack the liquidity and guarantee of the previous investments we've discussed. It's true a number of tax-free bonds are issued with insurance, but the insurance is issued by a private corporation. A private company is only as strong as its balance sheet. The concern over private of insurance was on full display in 2008 when a number of investments that were rated highly because of the insurance coverage performed poorly. The private insurance did little to protect investors from large losses.

Tax-free municipal bonds can increase your income, especially when compared to CDs and US Treasuries. For those investors looking to add a little more income to their accounts, we will now move on to corporate bonds.

CHAPTER 21

CORPORATE BONDS

*And God is able to bless you abundantly,
so that in all things at all times,
having all that you need you will
abound in every good work.*
—2 CORINTHIANS 9:8

Corporate bonds are issued by corporations—hence the term. These bonds are issued by companies needing or wanting to raise cash. They're backed by the companies issuing them and aren't guaranteed or backed by a taxing authority like municipal bonds are. Your corporate bond is only as safe as the company issuing it. If you own a bond issued by Walmart, it's going to be safe and predictable.

Most corporate bonds are rated by Standard & Poor's or Moody's, so you can easily compare the safety of two or more bonds. This first line of comparison is a good place to start when you're looking for corporate bonds to purchase. A triple-A-rated bond is going to be much safer to own than a bond with a rating of B-. The quality of the company will determine not only the rating but also the coupon rate. A bond with a triple-A-rating will typically have a lower coupon rate than a bond with a B-rating. A higher rating means less income. The rates can you expect to receive today are anywhere from below .25 percent to over 5 percent.

Corporate bonds aren't guaranteed and may have liquidity problems if the bond market falls apart, as it did in 2008. For this reason, it's not wise to rely solely on the rating agencies. You must do your homework. The balance sheet, income, and cash-flow statements will tell you all you need to know about the ability of a corporation to meet its debt obligations. I recommend spending some time reviewing the financials. A company with a strong balance sheet and solid cash flow is going to be a solid investment, while a company with weak financials will not.

Corporate bonds issue a prospectus or memorandum allowing you to review the offering and find out how the company is going to use the proceeds. The bond may be used to redeem debt issued in years past at a higher rate—similar to what you may do when you refinance your mortgage. A company may also issue debt for acquisitions or general corporate purposes. The more informed you are about the bond you're buying; the better investor you will become.

The interest on the bonds is taxable and can be held in taxable or retirement accounts. Interest on corporate bonds is paid every six months. Occasionally issuers pay monthly.

Corporate bonds trade in $1,000 increments and have maturities ranging from a few months to one hundred years. They offer a tremendous amount of flexibility and can be a nice addition to your account when matched with CDs, treasuries, and tax-free bonds.

The allocation on corporate bonds should be similar to tax-free municipal bonds. Thus, I recommend no more than 50 percent to 75 percent of your investment portfolio be allocated to bonds with an investment grade rating of BBB+ or better.

CHAPTER 22

STOCKS

> *The man became rich, and his
> wealth continued to grow until
> he became very wealthy.*
> —GENESIS 26:13

Stocks are purchased for growth. So why own them for income? Because stocks provide another powerful component most investors choose to ignore: the dividend. Dividend-paying stocks can be used to generate current and long-term income. A number of companies have a long history of paying and raising their dividends year in and year out. According to an article by Sam Ro of Business Insider, dividends have accounted for 42 percent of the stock-market return since 1930—almost half![40]

---

[40] *Dividends Were Responsible for 42% of Stock Market Returns Since 1930.*, Sam Ro, 1/10/2013, http://www.businessinsider.com/stock-returns-price-dividend-contribution-2013-1.

Standard & Poor's Dividend Aristocrats List is a useful resource for finding dividend-paying companies.[41] Companies on this list have raised their dividends every year for the past twenty-five years. These are solid companies with excellent track records and can be used to build a dividend-paying portfolio. Some of the companies in this elite group are Walmart, McDonald's, AT&T, Procter & Gamble, and Johnson & Johnson.

Another list for finding high-quality dividend-paying companies is the *Morningstar® Dividend Investor(SM)* newsletter authored by Josh Peters, CFA. The newsletter is for individuals looking for companies paying and growing their dividends. In the March 2016 issue, Mr. Peters references a study by Dartmouth Professor Kenneth French.[42] This study highlights the benefits of owning high-yielding dividend-paying stocks. Mr. French compares the returns of dividend-paying stocks across different deciles. A decile is ten sectors or classes so the study looked at dividend paying stocks across these different sectors.

In his study, the top 30 percent dividend-yielding stocks had an average annual total return of 12.4 percent from 1945 to 2015. How does this compare to non-dividend-paying companies? Non-dividend-paying stocks generated a total return of 8.8 percent per year during this same stretch. The highest dividend payers outperformed non-dividend payers by 3.6 percent per year!

---

41 S&P Dow Jones Indices, S&P 500 Dividend Aristocrats, http://us.spindices.com/indices/strategy/sp-500-dividend-aristocrats.

42 Kenneth R. French, *Morningstar® Dividend Investor(SM)*, March 2016, Vol. 12 No. 2, Morningstar Analysis.

UP THE INCOME LADDER

This is another reason to own dividend-paying stocks—to help you generate more income.

The dividend yields may appear low (2–4 percent), but strong companies often raise their dividends annually, if not more. Therefore, dividend-paying stocks with a long history of dividend increases are a way to generate both growth and income.

Below is a list of companies with a dividend yield north of 2 percent who have grown their dividends over 7 percent per year for five years. Looking at the list below, we see names like Microsoft, Pepsi, and McDonald's.

Microsoft has been a mainstay of America for many years. If in April of 2006 you had purchased $10,000 worth of Microsoft stock, ten years later it is worth $20,650, a gain of 106.5 percent. In the ten years you held the stock, you received $3,106 in dividend income. Microsoft's dividend has increased 17 percent per year for the past ten years.[43]

Let's look at Pepsi. In April of 2006, you might have purchased $10,000 of Pepsi stock. Ten years later, your investment is now worth $17,679. During this ten-year stretch, Pepsi has increased $7,679, or 76.79 percent, and you received over $3,439 in dividends. The Pepsi dividend has increased over 11.54 percent per year.[44]

Last, let's look at a thirty-year history of McDonald's. It has delivered solid returns to shareholders over the years. In April of 1986, you might have invested $10,000 in McDonald's stock. Thirty years later, your McDonald's

---
43 Morningstar Office® Tools Hypothetical Illustration.
44 Ibid.

investment would now be worth $228,585, and you would have received dividend income of $51,337! Your McDonald's investment has increased over twenty-two times, and your dividend income is more than five times your original investment.[45]

Here is the list of companies from the Value Line Investment Survey®:

Company Name	Ticker	Dividend Five-Year Growth Rate	Dividend Yield
3M Company	MMM	7	2.83%
Accenture Plc New	ACN	22	2.23%
Air Products and Chemicals Inc.	APD	10.5	2.47%
American Express Company	AXP	13	2.14%
Ameriprise Financial Inc.	AMP	25	3.18%
Applied Materials Inc.	AMAT	10	2.33%
Archer Daniels Midland Company	ADM	12.5	3.54%

---

45 Ibid.

Automatic Data Processing Inc.	ADP	9	2.50%
BlackRock Inc.	BLK	18	2.90%
Boeing Co	BA	7	3.71%
CA Inc.	CA	44.5	3.43%
Caterpillar Inc.	CAT	8.5	4.66%
Chevron Corporation	CVX	9.5	4.94%
CME Group Inc.	CME	16.5	2.63%
Coach Inc.	COH	54.5	3.72%
Coca-Cola Company	KO	8.5	3.21%
Colgate Palmolive Co	CL	11	2.26%
Cracker Barrel Old Country Store Inc.	CBRL	33	3.19%
Deere and Co	DE	14.5	2.99%
Discover Financial Services	DFS	37.5	2.41%
Exxon Mobil Corp	XOM	10	3.54%
Fastenal Co	FAST	25	2.69%
Franklin Resources Inc.	BEN	11	2.08%

Gap Inc.	GPS	14.5	3.51%
General Dynamics Corporation	GD	10	2.04%
General Mills Inc.	GIS	12	3.00%
Guess Inc.	GES	19.5	4.56%
Harris Corporation	HRS	17	2.69%
Honeywell International Inc.	HON	9	2.24%
Illinois Tool Works Inc.	ITW	7.5	2.30%
Intel Corporation	INTC	11.5	3.54%
International Business Machines Corp	IBM	15	3.93%
JM Smucker Company	SJM	12	2.10%
Johnson and Johnson	JNJ	7.5	2.88%
Johnson Controls Inc.	JCI	10	3.25%
Kimberly Clark Corp	KMB	7.5	2.84%

UP THE INCOME LADDER

Lockheed Martin Corp	LMT	20.5	3.08%
Mattel Inc.	MAT	13.5	4.83%
McDonalds Corp	MCD	12.5	3.04%
Mead Johnson Nutrition Company	MJN	31	2.21%
Medtronic plc	MDT	12	2.03%
MetLife Inc.	MET	7	3.83%
Microsoft Corporation	MSFT	17	2.76%
Nestle SA	NSRGY	13.5	3.18%
New Jersey Resources Corp	NJR	8.5	2.78%
Norfolk Southern Corp	NSC	10.5	3.15%
Novartis AG	NVS	9.5	3.62%
Omnicom Group Inc.	OMC	20.5	2.63%
Paychex Inc.	PAYX	8	3.30%
PepsiCo Inc.	PEP	7.5	2.82%
Polaris Industries Inc.	PII	18	2.55%
Praxair Inc.	PX	11	2.87%

Principal Financial Group Inc.	PFG	10.5	4.09%
Procter and Gamble Co	PG	8.5	3.23%
Public Storage	PSA	18	2.76%
Qualcomm Inc.	QCOM	18	3.91%
Ralph Lauren Corporation	RL	49	2.25%
Raytheon Co	RTN	13.5	2.20%
Rockwell Automation Inc.	ROK	14.5	2.85%
Schlumberger Ltd	SLB	11.5	2.75%
Siemens AG	SIEGY	13.5	3.99%
Stanley Black and Decker Inc.	SWK	9	2.38%
T Rowe Price Group Inc.	TROW	10	3.11%
Target Corp	TGT	21	3.09%
Teva Pharmaceutical Industries Ltd	TEVA	20	2.38%
Texas Instruments Incorporated	TXN	21.5	2.87%
The Travelers Companies Inc.	TRV	10.5	2.24%

Tiffany and Co	TIF	17	2.45%
Time Warner	TWX	9.5	2.49%
Tupperware Brands	TUP	20	5.45%
Union Pacific Corp	UNP	27.5	2.80%
United Parcel Service	UPS	7.5	3.20%
United Technologies Corporation	UTX	10	2.90%
V F Corp	VFC	10	2.42%
Walmart Stores Inc.	WMT	13	3.12%
Williams Sonoma	WSM	19.5	2.42%

Source: Value Line Investment Survey, Value Line: Smart research, Smarter Investing™

How much money should you allocate to stocks? I recommend setting your upper limit at no more than 80 percent to 90 percent of your portfolio. This doesn't mean you should go to the top of this range—but you could. An 80–90 percent allocation to stocks involves a high level of risk, but it may be worth the ride—especially if you have a time horizon of ten or more years.

CHAPTER 23

OPTIONS

*I have chosen the way of faithfulness;
I have set my heart on your laws.
—PSALM 119:30*

I first must say options involve risk and aren't suitable for all investors! This warning message is on all option forms and communication because it's true. Options do involve risk, and they aren't suitable for everyone—so why would you want to add options to your investment accounts? As with all investments, there are multiple sides to a trade and various ways to make money.

An option consists of a call or a put. Calls and puts can be bought or sold like any investment. In buying a call, you want your investment to appreciate in value. In selling a call, you want your investment to do nothing or go down slightly.

When you buy a put option, you want your investment to go down so that you can profit from the declining

UP THE INCOME LADDER

value of the underlying investment. When you sell a put option, you want your investment to appreciate.

If you're bullish, buy a call or sell a put. If you're bearish, buy a put or sell a call.

Whether they are puts or calls, options have some unique features. An option is a contract controlling one hundred shares of stock. It's a derivative of the underlying investment. If you want to control one thousand shares of stock, you'll need ten option contracts.

The option contract is a function of the stock price, time, and strike price. The option contract ends or expires on the expiration date, likely to be the third Friday of every month. Some companies have added options with weekly expirations. They can expire in a few days or a few years. The strike price is your target price.

Let's say Apple is currently trading at $110. We can pick a strike price near or far from this price. The option will trade in the money, at the money, or out of the money, depending on whether you are buying or selling a call or a put. For example, if we buy an Apple call option with a strike price of $115, this option is out of the money ($110 < $115). This same strike price on a purchase of a put option is in the money ($115 > $110). The reverse is true if we're selling the option. If we sold the Apple $115 call, we're out of the money ($110 < $115). The seller of the put on this trade would be in the money ($115 > $110). The strike price, the stock price, and the direction of our option will determine if we're in, at, or out of the money.

In buying a call option, you want the stock to rise. When you buy a call, you want the stock to go higher because of the leverage you employ by owning the option. You can buy one thousand shares of Apple (AAPL) at $110 and spend $110,000. If the option is priced at $5, you'd pay $5,000 (ten contracts at $5 per share). You're controlling the same number of shares, one thousand, with the stock and the option.

The five dollars is referred to as the option premium. It's what you pay or receive if you buy or sell an option.

Why spend $110,000 when you can own Apple for $5,000? Good question. The short answer is you can lose 100 percent of your $5,000 investment by purchasing the call option. How? When you buy a call option, you have to be right on the stock, price, time, and direction. If you're wrong in any one of these categories, you lose. The timing of the call option will play a huge part in whether you make or lose money.

On the other side of this Apple trade is the seller of the call option. When you sell an option, you don't really care what the stock does, because as soon as you sell your option, the premium is credited to your account. If you sold the Apple call instead of buying it, the $5,000 would credit your account on the day of the trade. The stock could go up, down, or sideways, and you would still retain the option premium.

To generate income for your portfolio, you want to be a seller of options. The first strategy is the buy-write or covered call. In this example you own one thousand shares of Microsoft. Let's say the price of Microsoft is $55. You sell the May 60 call. This is an out-of-the money call option, since you're selling the $60 strike and the price of Microsoft is $55 ($55 < $60). In this example, the option is currently bid at fifty cents and offered at fifty-five cents.

You're going to be a seller of the call option. You'll sell ten contracts on the bid, since you own one thousand shares of Microsoft (one contract = one hundred shares of stock). Again, the fifty cent bid is referred to as the option premium. The ten contracts will generate $500 in income (10 × .50 × 100). The $500 will credit your account on the day of your trade. If Microsoft stays below $60 on the third Friday in May, you'll keep it. If Microsoft trades above $60 on expiration, you're obligated to sell it at $60 regardless of how high above $60 Microsoft is trading. If Microsoft closed at $100 on expiration, you're still obligated to sell your stock at $60. You must forgo the $40 profit. The income from options is taxed as ordinary income, so it's best to sell calls in a tax-deferred account such as an IRA.

As a warning, never sell a call without owning the underlying stock position. This is considered an uncovered or naked call, and your risk exposure is unlimited. If you sell ten contracts on a $20 stock without owning the underlying position and the stock rises to $50 per share, you're obligated to sell it at $20 and buy the stock at $50 for a loss of $30 per share. This is a strategy you'd be wise to avoid.

The second of many ways to generate income from options is to sell a put option on stocks you want to own. This is similar to placing a limit order on a stock you want to purchase at a lower price—except you get paid to wait.

For example, if you want to buy a stock at $35 currently trading at $40, you can put in a limit order and wait for it to trade at $35 or lower. You won't get paid for placing a limit order.

When you sell a put, you're obligated to purchase the stock if it trades at or below the strike price. If you sell a May $50 put on Microsoft while it's selling for $55, you'll get a credit of fifty cents per contract. If you sell ten contracts, the credit is $500 (10 × .5 × 100). If Microsoft trades at or below $55 per share, you're obligated to purchase one thousand shares of MSFT at $55, regardless of how far the price of the stock trades below $55.

This strategy is reserved for investors with a higher tolerance for risk. It's also recommended you only sell a put option for the amount of cash you have available in your account. This is known as cash-covered put. For example, if you have $25,000 in cash, you can sell ten put contracts on a $25 stock.

The selling or writing of options will generate extra income for your accounts. If you own individual stocks, this could be a strategy for you.

Selling options is an addition to your account, so there will be no asset-allocation adjustments needed. This is similar to adding a swimming pool to your home. The pool is a nice addition, but it doesn't change anything structural about your home.

CHAPTER 24

PREFERRED STOCKS

What do you prefer?
—1 Corinthians 4:21

A preferred stock is another investment helping you generate higher income in retirement. It can be found on the corporate balance sheet between bonds and common stocks. The preferred label is from this pecking order because it's preferred to common shares. The preference comes in the form of investors receiving their dividends before the common-stock shareholder. In the event of a corporate liquidation, bondholders would be paid first, preferred holders second, and common-stock shareholders third.

A preferred stock is a hybrid between common stock and a corporate bond, which is why you'll get a higher dividend than you would from owning the common stock. In addition, you may get price appreciation. It's possible to invest in preferred stocks generating income of 6 percent or more.

Preferred stocks are, more often than not, issued at $25 per share. They may also be called, or redeemed, by the issuer after five years at $25 per share. However, with interest rates falling, they typically aren't being called.

The price of a preferred stock will stay close to the $25 price. If rates are falling, they may trade to $28 or $30 per share. When rates are rising, the price may fall to $20 or $21 per share. They're sensitive to interest rates, like bonds, and their price will adjust up or down based on the level of interest rates.

Preferred stocks are rated just like bonds, so make sure you invest in one with a quality rating. Standard & Poor's and Moody's will apply a rating from triple-A to D, depending on the quality of the issue. It's rare to find a triple-A-rated preferred stock; most preferred issues fall in the BB or B range. Ratings don't tell the whole story, as we found out in 2008. The balance sheet of the company also plays a part. During the Great Recession, a number of preferred stocks fell to single digits.

On the surface a preferred stock sounds like a solid investment. However, the devil is in the details. As I mentioned, most preferred stocks are called after five years. If you purchased a preferred stock with the intention of getting your money back after five years and it isn't called, you may have to hold your investment for many years. It's possible your five-year preferred would not be called and your short-term investment would turn into a thirty-, forty-, or fifty-year holding.

A preferred stock is sold with a prospectus, so you'll be able to see the details of the investment before you purchase, including the maturity date if it's not called after five years.

Of course, you can sell your investment at any time, but you may get more or less than your purchase price. This is a risk for investors in a rising-interest-rate environment. In a rising-interest-rate environment, a company isn't likely to redeem a lower-yielding investment and replace it with a higher-yielding investment.

Where can you find data on preferred stocks? *Barron's* has a tremendous section with a long list of preferred stocks. In the stock tables, you'll be able to look for investments by name, price, yield, and so on. Once you have identified a few names, you can do further research online.

An allocation of 5–10 percent of your account to this investment will give your fixed-income portfolio a boost.

CHAPTER 25

REAL-ESTATE INVESTMENT TRUSTS

Yet it did not fall, because it had its foundation on the rock.
—MATTHEW 7:25

Location, location, location. How often have you heard that saying? Real estate has been a popular investment for many and a wealth creator for generations. Most investors like real estate because it's tangible and generates income.

My grandfather used to tell me he never lost money in real estate and it had always treated him well. I told him real estate did well for individuals because the values of their homes weren't broadcast daily on CNBC like stocks are. Can you imagine watching a ticker and seeing the value of your home rise or fall by $50,000 or more per day?

UP THE INCOME LADDER

People need places to live, and most stay in their home for a decade or more.[46] Stock investors are not as patient, with holding periods counted in months rather than years.[47] Would you want to buy a home every nineteen months?

Rental property is a popular investment for individuals looking for income. In addition, the opportunity to make money from price appreciation is another reason to own rental property. However, the cost to purchase rental property may be prohibitive for many. Taking care of multiple properties can also be a barrier for those looking to manage a portfolio of homes.

An answer to buying individual properties is a real-estate investment trust (REIT). A REIT is a publicly traded investment that owns property and mortgages. The property owned can be apartment complexes, malls, commercial buildings, and mortgages. By law, a REIT must pay out 90 percent of its income to shareholders.[48] This high payout is one reason to own this asset class.

The income from a REIT is why you may want to consider adding them to your portfolio. The investment return in this category has treated investors well over the years. The Vanguard Real Estate Invest Trust Index (VNQ) has averaged 9.64 percent for the past

---

46 *Latest Study Shows Average Buyer Expected to Stay in a Home 13 Years.*, Paul Emrath, 1/3/2013, http://eyeonhousing.org/2013/01/latest-study-shows-average-buyer-expected-to-stay-in-a-home-13-years/.

47 *Why Hair-Trigger Traders Lose the Race,* Jason Zweig, 4/10/2015, http://blogs.wsj.com/moneybeat/2015/04/10/why-hair-trigger-stock-traders-lose-the-race/.

48 Investopedia definition Real Estate Trust (REIT), http://www.investopedia.com/terms/r/reit.asp.

twelve years. A $10,000 investment in 2004 is now worth $28,880.[49] The current yield for VNQ is 4.21 percent.

The corresponding REIT index is the National Association of Real Estate Investment Trusts (NAREIT).

Allocating 5–10 percent of your assets to this sector is an appropriate amount for your account.

---

49 Morningstar Office® Tools Hypothetical Illustration

CHAPTER 26

ANNUITIES

*I have received full payment and
have more than enough.*
—PHILIPPIANS 4:18

Having guaranteed income for life helps eliminate a number of problems individuals may face in their retirement years.

Guaranteed income used to be a corporate benefit, but it's no longer available for most individuals. It was not uncommon to work for a company with multiple retirement benefits, one being a pension plan.

Responsibility for retirement income has shifted from the employer to the employee, so how can you add a guaranteed income for your retirement? The tax-deferred annuity is an investment with the ability to deliver guaranteed income for life.

An annuity is a contract between you and an insurance company. When you invest in annuity, it will generate income for as long as you're living. You can also turn this income into lifetime payments for your spouse. The joint and survivor option allows you to guarantee income for both lives, so you each have the opportunity to enjoy the income.

An annuity may be appropriate for individuals with a lower level of assets who need to generate a certain amount of income to meet their needs. The guaranteed fixed payments from the annuity may be your best option to cover your everyday living expenses. It can also be used by those who have a substantial amount of assets and want to cover their fixed expenses with the cash flow, letting the remainder of their investments grow.

There are a few downsides to the annuity. One is the income isn't indexed to inflation. Your annuity will provide you a fixed payment for life but will never adjust upward to reflect the cost of living increases.

For example, your fixed annuity will pay $5,000 per month for the rest of your life. This $5,000 is fixed forever but not indexed to inflation. This means in twenty-five years the purchasing power of your $5,000 fixed-annuity payment will drop to an inflation-adjusted number of $2,388.02, a 52 percent drop in real income (twenty-five years of 3 percent inflation). However, most insurance companies will give you the option to purchase an inflation rider, allowing your income to rise with the cost of living. When you add an inflation rider or other riders to an annuity, it will increase the cost of ownership, lowering your income.

Another negative to owning an annuity is the cost. It includes a number of components like the mortality and expenses (M&E), surrender charges, investment management fees, and riders. The cost of an annuity can run as high as 3 percent, which isn't cheap.[50] The Mortality and expenses usually cover the insurance, commission and expenses for the annuity.

The surrender charge is worth considering. The surrender charge is a back-end deferred sales charge. When you buy an annuity, there isn't a front-in sales charge, so 100 percent of your money will go to work for you right away. However, if you need to sell, you may be forced to pay a deferred sales charge of 7 percent or more. The deferred sales charge will decline over the years. In the first year, the sales charge to liquidate may be 7 percent. The following year it'll drop to 6 percent, and then 5 percent, 4 percent, and so on. If you needed your money in year two, you may have to pay a penalty of 6 percent or more to get it.

There are a number of ways to get income from your annuity. You can receive monthly or annual income based on the current rate offered by the insurance company. This rate will be in line with current interest rates you can obtain from other income-producing investments. You can annuitize your payments.

Annuitization allows you to receive monthly income for a certain period of time or life. When you annuitize your

---

50 *How much do annuities cost?* Office of the Insurance Commissioner, Washington State, updated 3/27/2014, https://www.insurance.wa.gov/your-insurance/annuities/understanding-annuities/how-much-do-annuities-cost/.

annuity, the insurance company will send you a check with a combination of income and principal. The income component will be taxed as ordinary income. Annuitization is similar to turning on the faucet in your kitchen sink and then ripping off the handles, because once you start to receive the income, it can't be turned off.

The other factor with annuitization is your money will be gone when you're gone unless you opt for a "period certain." If you expect to receive guaranteed income for twenty years, but you pass away after you receive your first payment, game over. The money you invested in the annuity will now revert to the insurance company unless you decided to receive the payments for a period certain. A period certain can be ten years, which means your beneficiaries will receive payments after you pass away during the ten-year period-certain window.

For example, you purchase an annuity at age sixty for $100,000, and based on the current interest rate, you'll receive $450 per month for the rest of your life. After receiving your first $450, you get hit by a bus. The remainder of your annuity will now be an asset of the insurance company. In this situation, you lose, and the insurance company wins. The opposite can also happen. You may live to one hundred twenty and receive payments worth $324,000 ($450 × 12 × 60). In this case, you win, and the insurance company loses. If you chose a ten-year period certain, your beneficiaries will receive the remainder of your payments for ten years.[51]

---

51 *Is Annuitization Your Best Strategy?* Mark P. Cussen, CFP®, CMFC, AFC, updated 5/28/2014, http://www.investopedia.com/articles/personal-finance/052714/annuitization-your-best-strategy.asp.

An annuity can replace your fixed-income allocation if you're looking for guaranteed income. If you're willing to give up some liquidity for guaranteed income, you can allocate up to 100 percent of your assets into an annuity. This piece of your portfolio can provide you with an income lift needed later on in your retirement years.

Annuities are expensive, so weigh the cost to purchase versus your peace of mind. I recommend using an annuity only as a last resort due to the high cost and low liquidity.

CHAPTER 27

BENCHMARKS

See, I lay a stone in Zion, a tested stone, a precious cornerstone for a sure foundation; the one who relies on it will never be stricken with panic.
—ISAIAH 28:16

In the 1980 classic golf movie *Caddyshack*, Ty Webb, played by Chevy Chase, is asked by Judge Smells, played by Ted Knight, what he shot on the golf course. Ty responded, "Oh, Judge, I don't keep score."

Judge Smells asks, "Then how do you measure yourself with other golfers?"

Ty responds, "By height."[52] A great scene in a great movie. These two famous characters had different measures for benchmarks.

---

52 IMDb Caddyshack (1980) Quotes, http://www.imdb.com/title/tt0080487/quotes.

A benchmark is a standard, or point of reference, in measuring or judging quality or value.[53] A benchmark is also used by surveyors as a reference point.

As you construct your investment portfolio, you'll want to pay attention to your securities and compare apples to apples when you're looking at performance. The most common benchmark is the Standard & Poor 500 index. This is "the market." The S&P 500 is one of the most recognized indices in the world. However, is it the right benchmark for your portfolio? It's likely you own a diversified portfolio of large, small, and international stocks. You may also own bonds of various types like CDs, government bonds, tax-free bonds, high-grade corporate bonds, junk bonds, and international bonds. In addition, you might have some exposure to alternative investments like real estate, gold, wheat, oil, or some other commodity.

As you can see, if you have a diversified portfolio, you'll have more than one benchmark with which to compare your holdings. If you relied solely on the S&P 500 index to see how you are doing, you'll give yourself a false sense of hope or security. It's possible when the US stock market is up, your other investments could be down and vice versa. In a diversified account you may only have 10 percent to 15 percent of your investments in large, US companies, while the remainder of your account has nothing to do with the S&P 500.

This scenario played out in 2014. Large companies in the United States did very well, but other asset classes did

---

[53] *Merriam-Webster* Collegiate® Dictionary, Eleventh Edition.

not. The DJIA and the S&P 500 generated double-digit returns. The Dow was up 13 percent and the S&P was up 14 percent. It's unlikely you had 100 percent of your assets in these two indices. Some clients weren't happy with their return on their accounts because they *only* made 6 percent or 7 percent. I explained to them in 2014 large companies did well, but the other categories could not keep pace. Large, developed international companies as measured by the MSCI EAFE index were down over 6 percent while US bonds and US small company stocks were up about 6 percent. And, as you know, cash paid nothing. If you had a diversified portfolio of large, small, and international companies with a pinch of bonds and cash, it wasn't possible to generate double-digit returns in 2014.

Years ago, while working for Dean Witter in Pasadena, California, I had a client with 100 percent of his money invested in CDs, corporate bonds, and US Treasuries. On most Monday mornings he'd call and ask what I thought the stock market was going to do for the week. He wanted to know if we should make any changes to his account. I'd remind him his account had nothing to do with the stock market, and his investments would be fine regardless if the market went up or down. He was programmed to believe if the stock market was doing well, then so was he.

Another client was looking at a basket of investment choices, and he only wanted an advisor who was outperforming the S&P 500. He told me as long as the money manager beat the stock market, he didn't care how they handled his money. This reminds me of Will Rogers's quote on stock ownership: "Don't gamble; take all your savings and buy some good stock and hold it till it goes up, then sell it. If it don't go up, don't buy it."

So how should you construct your benchmark? How do you know if you're doing well or not? How will you know if you're staying ahead of your goals or falling behind? A baseline for your account is paramount. A quick review of your portfolio asset allocation will be the starting point in constructing your benchmark. The creation of your benchmark will be easy once your asset allocation is determined. Your personal benchmark will give you a better picture of how your investments are holding up. For example, if you have 50 percent in large US stocks, 30 percent in small US stocks, and 20 percent in US Treasury bonds, you can create an index with the S&P 500, the Russell 2000, and the Barclays US Treasury Index. Your index will give you a stronger reading of how well you're doing more so than the isolated S&P 500 benchmark.

Besides using traditional market benchmarks, you can also gauge your investments against inflation or the cost of living index. The main inflation index is the Consumer Price Index, or CPI. Are your investments keeping pace with inflation and the cost of living? This is an easy calculation, as you're only comparing your portfolio total return with the CPI Index. If your investments are outpacing inflation, you're doing well.

In 2011 I ran the Boston Marathon. I knew going into the race I wasn't going to win nor was I going to come in last. I couldn't worry about the lead runners and what their pace was going to be. If I tried to compare myself to their split and finishing times, I'd have felt like my race was a total loss. Instead, I charted a course to finish the race consistent with my own personal record performance. I was one of about thirty thousand runners on race day, but I was only concerned with my time. I knew where I had to be at each mile to achieve my goal. As a result, I finished the race faster than expected and set a personal record. My benchmark worked for me and what I was trying to achieve. I ran the race in 3:22.01 for a new personal record.

CHAPTER 28

Portfolio Construction

*If what has been built survives, the
builder will receive a reward.*
—1 Corinthians 3:14

"Keep it simple" should be your theme when it comes to constructing your portfolio, simple and easy to understand. If it's too complicated and you don't understand what you own, you're less likely to hold your investments for the long haul. If you don't hold your investments for the long term, you may miss an opportunity to create generational wealth. Also, if your investments are keeping you up at night because they're too complicated or risky, sell them and buy ones more in line with your financial goals. There are too many quality investments for you to pick from, so don't waste your time owning ones causing you heartache. You don't need complicated investments or investment strategies to generate income or create long-term returns.

As I said earlier, I prefer to use individual investments and low-cost index funds because of their clarity and cost structure. Thanks to the simplicity of these investments, I'm in a better position to track their returns and spend more time on my financial goals. In addition, the costs can be controlled and the fees are minimal.

How and where should you start when constructing your portfolio? The starting point should be your financial plan. It'll be your blueprint for building your portfolio. The financial plan will give you the best guidance for the allocation you choose and the investments you'll own to achieve your goal. If your plan calls for a longer term, more growth oriented time horizon, then you want to own more stocks than bonds. A portfolio tilted toward stocks will give you the best opportunity for achieving your long-term goals.

Let's say a fifty-year-old with current assets of $200,000 has a goal to accumulate $1 million by age sixty-five. She is willing to invest $15,000 per year. Her target growth rate is 7.64 percent, calling for more stocks than bonds.

On the other hand, if her plan is more conservative, then she should own more bonds than stocks. Bonds will give her more predictable and stable returns. A portfolio built on bonds will be more conservative than one with stock exposure. If it's worth $1 million at age sixty-five, she'd want to reduce her stock allocation and buy more bonds. She has achieved her goal, so there's no need to take on additional risk.

When constructing your masterpiece, it's wise to maintain realistic expectations. In a world where the thirty-year US Treasury Bond is yielding less than 2.75 percent, don't expect to generate income of 15 percent. Nor should you expect to double your money every year. A realistic outlook will give you much needed peace of mind as you generate income or grow your account. If your financial plan calls for outlandish numbers and targets, you need to go back to the drawing board and make some adjustments.

Let's take a short detour before we look at the portfolio models. If you're an investor in need of a little excitement in your life, I recommend investing up to 5 percent of your assets in investments that carry a higher level of risk. This can be the speculation component of your account. With a 5 percent allocation to high-risk strategies, it shouldn't bring the house down if your investment strategy goes awry. Let's compare this to two puzzles. If you have a two-piece puzzle and you lose one of the pieces, what do you have? It's hard to imagine a one-piece puzzle. If you lose one piece from a one-thousand-piece puzzle, it's no big deal. You still have 999 pieces left, and you can still tell what the puzzle is supposed to look like.

Now, let's look at a few model portfolio returns based on the Ibbotson SBBI 2015 Classic Year Book. The returns cover eighty-eight years of returns from 1926 to 2014. We'll look at three allocation models. They own two asset classes—stocks and bonds. When you're constructing your portfolio, you should own multiple asset classes like large, small, and international companies; emerging markets, real estate, bonds, and cash. However, the examples below will give you a view of risk versus return.

Portfolio 1 = 90 percent stocks and 10 percent bonds. The average return for this allocation was 9.6 percent, and it made money 73 percent of the time. The best year was 1933 with a gain of 49.03 percent, and the worst year was 1931 with a loss of 39.73 percent. The standard deviation, risk level, was 18.1 percent, which means the normal range for this portfolio fell between a positive 28.20 percent and a negative 8 percent. (18.1 + 10.1 = 28.2; 10.1 − 18.1 = -8).

Portfolio 2 = 50 percent stocks and 50 percent bonds. The average return for this allocation was 8.3 percent. It made money 78 percent of the time. The best year was 1995 with a gain of 34.71 percent, and the worst year was 1931 with a loss of 24.7 percent. The standard deviation, risk level, was 11.2 percent, which means the normal range for this portfolio fell between a positive 19.66 percent and a negative 2.74. (11.2 + 8.46 = 19.66; 8.46 − 11.2 = -2.74).

Portfolio 3 = 10 percent stocks and 90 percent bonds. The average return for this allocation was 6.3 percent. It made money 78 percent of the time. The best year was 1982 with a gain of 38.48 percent, and the worst year was 2009 with a loss of

11.23 percent. The standard deviation, risk level, was 9.2 percent, which means the normal range for this portfolio fell between a positive 15.48 percent and a negative 2.92. (9.2 + 6.28 = 15.48; 6.28 − 9.2 = -2.92).

Today there are no shortages of model portfolios you can follow, and they can be found online from a variety of websites. If you're not sure where to start in constructing your portfolio, you can follow the direction of any of these models. Your advisor can also help design a model portfolio in line with your financial goals.

The foundation for your portfolio construction will be your financial plan. Can you imagine trying to build a home, an airplane, or a bridge without a blueprint? Your financial plan will be your blueprint.

CHAPTER 29

MR. MARKET

*I, wisdom, dwell together with prudence;
I possess knowledge and discretion.*
—PROVERBS 8:12

What about Mr. Market? Should you be concerned with the day-to-day gyrations in the stock market? I guess you should if you're a day trader. The market has a mind of its own, and it will do what it wants to do.

Mr. Market[54] is a term coined by Benjamin Graham, the legendary investor who wrote *The Intelligent Investor*. He said Mr. Market is full of emotion and sometimes doesn't make much sense to the true investor.

The stock market, in the short term, can ignite extreme fear to passionate euphoria. This is good and bad. A stock market bouncing around a lot and making

---

54 Investopedia definition, Mr. Market, http://www.investopedia.com/terms/m/mr-market.asp.

international headlines isn't good for the psyche of the investor. The short-term gyrations force people to remove their eyeballs from their long-term goals and make investment decisions not in their best interest. As Warren Buffett once said, "The stock market is a device for transferring money from the impatient to the patient."

In the short term, the return on your investments will be a flip of a coin. I have said stocks only go down twice. The first time your stocks will go down is right after you buy them, and the second time is when you need the money. At all other times the stock market is rising.

If you're concerned about movement in the market, add bonds and cash to your portfolio. The more bonds and cash you add to your account, the less volatile it'll become, and the more conservative the ride, as we learned from the previous chapter. It also means your long-term returns will be less than a portfolio heavily dependent on stocks. The stock market for the long haul is the best way for you to build wealth. I recommended you hitch your goals and dreams to this long and glorious ride.

When to sell? If you need your money in one year or less. According to Morningstar and Ibbotson, the stock market has made money 73 percent of the time on a one-year basis between the years 1926 and 2014. However, this range is wide. The best year was 1933 with a gain of 53.99 percent and the worst year was 1931 with a loss of 43.34 percent.[55]

---

[55] *Market Results for Stocks, Bonds, Bills and Inflation 1926 – 2014.* Morningstar ® Ibbotson®SBBI® 2015 Classic Yearbook, page 49.

If you're going to buy something with the money invested in the stock market, sell. If you are going to buy a home, car, boat, or plane, then this money should be safely stored in cash.

If you have to pay for an event like a wedding or a college education, sell. My daughter is leaving the nest soon and heading off to college. Knowing a tuition payment is imminent, I liquidated half of her investment account two years ago and invested the proceeds in US Treasuries. I didn't want to have 100 percent stock exposure before she left for college.

Retiring in three to five years? Sell. You don't need to sell all of your stocks, just enough to cover three years' worth of household expenses. For example, if your annual household expenses are $100,000, you should have at least $300,000 in cash in your retirement or investment accounts.

Got debt? Selling assets to pay off your debt is a good idea. Debt is debt, and the less you owe, the better. A rule of thumb is your total monthly debt payments should be less than 36 percent of your gross income. For example, if your gross income is $10,000 per month, your total-debt payments should be no more than $3,600.[56]

Do you have a financial plan? If you don't, it's like driving a car without a steering wheel or sailing a ship without a rudder. How can you invest your hard-earned assets if you have no idea where you are going? A financial plan will help guide your investments and make you

---

56 *Savings Fitness: A Guide to your Money and your Financial Future.* https://www.cfp.net/docs/consumer-outreach-library/savings-fitness-guide.pdf?sfvrsn=6.

a better investor. A well-constructed financial plan will be your life guide.

Are you 100 percent invested in stocks? Reducing your stock exposure may be prudent. An all-stock portfolio had an average annual return of 10.1 percent with a standard deviation of 20.1 from 1926 to 2014. A portfolio invested in 70 percent stocks and 30 percent in bonds had an annual return of 9.2 percent and a standard deviation of 14.3. The addition of bonds to your account reduced your risk by 29 percent and your returns by .9 percent per year.[57]

If you don't fall into one of the above categories, buy stocks!

Again, I must point back to your financial plan. When Mr. Market is losing value or not acting rationally, your plan will help guide you through the valley. It will allow you to be a patient investor.

---

[57] *Market Results for Stocks, Bonds, Bills and Inflation 1926 – 2014.* Morningstar ® Ibbotson®SBBI® 2015 Classic Yearbook, page 50.

CHAPTER 30

MONEY MANAGEMENT

*Do not conform to the patterns of this world,
but be transformed by the
renewing of your mind.*
—ROMANS 12:12

To fee or not to fee, that is the question. The standard fee for asset management by an investment firm or professional is 1 percent. The 1 percent fee is based on the level of your assets. An account worth $1 million would have an annual fee of $10,000. It's deducted from your account on a quarterly basis, so each quarter you will see a fee for $2,500. The asset-management fee is applied to your account whether your account goes up or down. My fee, for the record, is 0.5 percent.

I've noticed when the market is at the extremes, either up significantly or down substantially, that is when people tend to question the fee the most. When the stock market is up 20 percent or more, investors probably think they can manage the money themselves and therefore don't need to pay a management fee of 1 percent. Equally, when the stock market is getting smoked, like it did in 2008, investors may say they could lose money on their own without paying a fee to have someone do it for them.

Should you pay a fee to have somebody manage your money? The answer is pretty simple. Do you like managing your money? Are you good at it? Do you have the time, interest, or discipline? Does managing your money get in the way of your day job or family life? With an honest answer, you should have a clear picture as to whether you can, or want, to have your assets managed.

If you're comfortable with making investment decisions on your own and don't need advice or guidance from a professional, by all means give it a go. If you're not at ease with managing your assets, hire a professional money manager or advisor. Investing is not a game. The cost of making a major mistake on your own will far outweigh any fee you pay an advisor.

CHAPTER 31

DIY INVESTING

You should mind your own business and work with your hands, just as we told you.
—*1 Thessalonians 4:10–13*

Managing your investment portfolio is analogous to gardening. Do you want a nice yard? To have a nice yard, you have to mow the lawn, trim the hedges, and pull the weeds. It's a year-round job, as you know if you've ever ignored your yard for a few weeks. So, too, must your investment portfolio be tended to on a regular basis. The grass must be trimmed, and the weeds must be pulled.

It's important to remove the weeds from your account. If you have a stock that isn't doing well, it must be sold and replaced with a better investment. For example, if you plant five rosebushes and one of them dies, you don't remove the four living ones and hope the fifth one is resurrected. You are much better off taking out the dead rosebush and planting a new one.

Trimming your portfolio requires you to rebalance your account on a regular basis. What does rebalancing mean? If you have a portfolio of stocks and bonds with an asset allocation of 50 percent stocks and 50 percent bonds at the beginning of the year, it's likely your account won't have the same percentage split at the end of the year.

Let's say you build a portfolio with 50 percent invested in IVV (iShares Core S&P 500 Index ETF) and TLT (iShares 20+Year Treasury Bond ETF). In a rising stock market, it's possible IVV will outperform TLT, and, as a result, your allocation now could be 60 percent in IVV and 40 percent in TLT. Your original allocation has strayed from the 50 percent/50 percent portfolio, and it may carry too much risk. Now it's time to rebalance, or trim, your portfolio. In your portfolio, you'd sell 10 percent of IVV and buy TLT with the proceeds. You're selling stocks and buying bonds to move your asset allocation back to 50 percent/50 percent. Rebalancing can be done as often as you like, but once or twice a year is probably all you'll need.

A hypothetical report on these two investments dating back to 2002 would have generated an average annual return of 7.66 percent. The allocation in 2002 was 50/50, but on January 31, 2016, the allocation was 57 percent stocks and 43 percent bonds. If you rebalanced this portfolio every year so you maintained 50 percent in IVV and 50 percent in TLT, you would have actually made more money with a return of 8.21 percent while at the same time keeping your risk exposure in line with your goals and expectations.[58]

To rebalance a portfolio with two investments is easy, but when you add multiple asset classes, it starts to get challenging. Let's look at your original portfolio starting off with 50 percent in IVV and 50 percent in TLT. Now add the following asset classes: small companies, international companies, emerging markets, short-term bonds, high-yield bonds, real-estate companies, high-grade corporate bonds, inflation-protected investments, mid-cap companies, commodities, gold, and large-company growth stocks. You now own multiple positions across multiple sectors. They include large, small, and international stocks along with a few different bond categories. The new account added commodities and real estate as well. You now own fourteen different investments. To rebalance this portfolio, it helps to have a spreadsheet showing your original allocation or a software program allowing you to rebalance online. An automatic or systematic rebalancing plan does take some emotion out of your buy and sell decisions.

Rebalancing may not increase your return, but it will reduce your risk.[59] For some it doesn't make sense to sell an investment doing well and buy one that isn't. This

---

58 Morningstar Office® Online Tools Hypothetical: IVV and TLT from July 22, 2002, to January 31, 2016; no taxes or fees were deducted.

59 Rebalancing: A strategy for reducing exposure to risk. Schwab Center for Financial Research, December 2015, http://content.schwab.com/web/retail/public/lookdeeper/rebalancing-strategy-reducing.html.

strategy is hard for people to grasp. It does have its roots in buy low and sell high, however.

The psychology of investing plays a huge part in how you manage your assets. During your working years, your investments were probably handled for you automatically through your company-retirement plan. The investments, asset allocation, and dollar amount were likely set to autopilot. This may have been true for your personal investments as well. Now that you're retired, you have the opportunity to manage your own money or work with an advisor who can help you achieve your financial goals.

The good news is you don't have to choose sides as to who will manage your money. You can do a combination of the two—self-directed and managed. This may give you the best of both worlds.

I once worked with a gentleman who had a strong financial background, and he was looking forward to managing his own money once he retired. After he retired, he consolidated his assets, and the sum was very large. The dollar amount was above his comfort zone, so we divided up the account so he managed a portion, and the remainder was managed by an investment firm.

CHAPTER 32

ADVISORS

*Serve wholeheartedly, as if you
the Lord, not people.*
—EPHESIANS 6:7

Deciding on a firm or an individual to handle your money can be almost as important as choosing the correct investments. Your choices for hiring an advisor are almost unlimited. It's important to know the difference between a broker and an advisor.

An advisor is a fiduciary who, per the Investment Advisors Act of 1940, must put your interest first. A Registered Investment Advisor (RIA)[60] works for the client. Most Registered Investment Advisors are self-employed individuals who work for an eponymous firm and are paid a percentage of assets, a flat fee, or an hourly rate.

---

60 Investopedia definition Registered Investment Advisor (RIA), http://www.investopedia.com/terms/r/ria.asp.

An RIA will provide you with their ADV form, highlighting their education, how they conduct their business, and how his fees are assessed. A registered investment advisor is paid for advice, not transactions. An advisor has little interest in generating transactions in your account because he isn't compensated by buying and selling investments. An advisor with assets of $100 million or more must register with the Securities and Exchange Commission (SEC).[61] An advisor with less than $100 million will register with his home state.

Advisors typically do not hold your assets at their firm. Assets managed on your behalf are held at a third-party custodian like TD Ameritrade or Fidelity. These firms will hold your investments and handle the back-office activity for your advisor. This is important because it will provide you another level of protection for your investments. You'll get monthly statements from the custodian in addition to performance reports and account detail from your advisor. You will be able to compare the two to make sure all the i's are dotted and the t's are crossed.

Registered investment advisors provide an open architecture platform. An open architecture for an RIA means your advisor can offer you investments from a number of different firms. It allows your advisor to offer you the best investment choices regardless of the company. Your advisor is not held captive to one fund company. The role of the advisor is to offer you advice and invest your assets in the most prudent way for your circumstances.

---

61 Division of Investment Management; Electronic Filing for Investment Advisors IARD, https://www.sec.gov/iard.

A broker usually works for a brokerage firm and is paid for transactions.[62] Most brokerage firms have a manufacturing division where they pump out products for their sales force to peddle to their clients. The products are typically mutual funds or insurance products. The firms manufacturing these products will make money when they are sold to you through their brokers.

Broker-sold funds may also have higher fees (expense ratios and 12b-1 fees) when compared to index funds. A 12b-1 is a marketing fee for the fund company. Brokers are paid on a commission, which may be a conflict of interest when they sell you a company-branded product. Brokers do not act in a fiduciary manner and only have to do what is suitable for your current situation. A broker does not have an obligation to find you the best investment at the lowest price. Brokers are registered under FINRA (Financial Industry Regulatory Authority) and will hold a Series 7 and other licenses, allowing them to work with clients and offer them a variety of investments.[63]

As you decide on which type of advisor to use, you'll want to ask a few questions. Here are some of the questions you can ask a broker or advisor:[64]

- How do you get paid?
- What does your fee include?
- What is your experience?
- What products or services do you offer?

---

62 Investopedia definition Broker, http://www.investopedia.com/terms/b/broker.asp.
63 http://www.finra.org/.
64 https://www.sec.gov/investor/pubs/askquestions.htm.

- Are you a fiduciary?
- Are you a Certified Financial Planner practitioner (CFP)?
- How do you invest your own money?
- Do you issue an investment policy statement?
- Do you offer financial planning?
- Will I receive a copy of your ADV?

This is a short list of questions. The more you ask, the better informed you'll be before you hire an advisor to work with you and your family.

CHAPTER 33

THE MECHANICS OF MOVING MONEY

The Lord has done it this very day;
let us rejoice today and be glad.
—PSALM 118:24

For the past forty years, you've been a worker bee and super saver. While working, you most likely contributed a portion of your pay to your company 401(k) plan, IRA, or investment accounts. Now what? Yesterday you were working, and today you're retired. Your savings train has finally arrived at your destination, and now it's time to disembark and start enjoying the fruits of your labor.

A common question from recent retirees is, "How do I take money out of my retirement accounts?" The process of moving money from your retirement accounts to your mailbox is simple. Money inside your accounts can be sent to you monthly, quarterly, annually, or as needed. The income-distribution options are limitless.

An easy option is to pay out the dividends and interest payments credited to your account during a particular month and receive a combined check for the total. During a certain month, you may receive dividends and income from various sources on different days. At the end of the month, we can total the amount you received and send you one check. This is a simple solution on how to get money from your account. However, your income will be sporadic and vary from month to month, especially if you own a large quantity of stocks and bonds.

The second option is to pay 'em as you get 'em, which means to pay your dividend and interest payments as soon as they credit your account. If you receive a dividend from Pepsi today, we'll send you a check tomorrow. This option is rarely chosen.

The option most often chosen by a retiree is to pay a flat dollar amount regardless of the amount your account generates in a particular month. For example, let's say you want to receive $5,000 per month from your retirement account. At the beginning of each month, you'd receive a $5,000 check regardless of how much income your investments generated. This is a popular strategy because it helps with the budgeting process.

Most people will opt to have their money electronically transferred and credited to their bank account from their brokerage or IRA account through the ACH channel. ACH stands for automated clearinghouse.[65]

The mechanics of moving money from your company-sponsored 401(k) or other company-retirement plan to an IRA is also an easy process. The money inside your company-sponsored retirement plan has been added through an automatic draft from your paycheck every pay period. The process of contributing money to your company-sponsored retirement plan was easy, seamless, and automated. Your investments inside your plan were probably automated as well with various percentages sent to a basket of mutual funds while having your dividends and capital gains reinvested. At retirement you'll start withdrawing money from your retirement plan to meet your needs.

The first suggestion is to roll over your company-retirement plan to an IRA account. This process is straightforward. The transfer will happen on a trustee to trustee basis so you shouldn't have to pay any fees, penalties, or taxes. Your corporate trustee will transfer the money to your new IRA custodian.

To start the rollover process, you'll need to contact your employer. The employer will give you a form or direct you to a website to complete the rollover process. Your company custodian will require you to have an IRA account number and address for your new custodian. Once the information is entered with your employer's custodian, the rollover will be processed and transferred to your IRA.

---

[65] Dictionary.com, http://www.dictionary.com/browse/automated-clearinghouse.

Why would you want to roll over your money to an IRA? Why not leave it in your company plan? The short answer is you don't have to roll over your company plan. If you're happy with your corporate-retirement plan, you can leave your money with your former employer. However, one of the main reasons for an IRA rollover is you'll have more investment choices in an IRA than are usually available to you through your company plan.

What if you want to cash out of your plan and receive a nice big check so you don't have to deal with the IRA rollover? A lump-sum payout is an option as well. Not a very wise option, but one option nevertheless.

Let's say your current 401(k) balance is $1 million, and you decide to cash out completely and receive a lump-sum check. What next? This distribution would be taxable at the state and federal levels as income. If you live in California, then 50.9 percent (39.6 percent for federal and 11.3 percent for state) of this distribution would be sent to the IRS for taxes.

What about taxes? When you remove your money from a traditional IRA account or other tax-deferred retirement plan, you'll owe taxes on the distribution based on your income tax bracket. If you receive $5,000 a month or $60,000 per year, your income will mirror this distribution amount. You'll receive a 1099-R showing the income you've received for the past calendar year. Taxes can be withheld from each distribution so you don't have to write one big check to the IRS in April.

Let's revisit the $5,000 distribution. After much thought you decide to have 20 percent withheld from each check to cover your taxes. You'll receive a net check for $4,000, and the other $1,000 will be sent to the IRS. At the end of the year, your distributions totaled $60,000 with $48,000 being sent to you and $12,000 to the IRS. You can have the check either way, gross or net; just remember the IRS will always get their share!

CHAPTER 34

SUMMARY

> *Well done, good and faithful servant! You have been faithful with a few things; I will put you in charge of many things. Come and share your master's happiness!*
> —MATTHEW 25:21

Thank you for reading my investment book. I hope I was able to help strengthen your financial situation and answer some of your questions. It's important your plan be *your* plan. You have to be comfortable with your investment- and asset-allocation choices in order to achieve your long-term goals. If you're comfortable with your plan and investments, good things will happen.

I recommend you review your financial plan on an annual basis to make sure it's still in line with your goals and your dreams. An annual birthday review is a good time to take inventory of your investments to make sure they are still in line with your short, intermediate, and long-term goals. Your watchful eye on your investments will help guide you to your financial promised land.

A few closing thoughts and reminders are as follows:

- Give big. With the fruits of your labor, you're in a position to help others who are in need. Your wealth, regardless of how many zeros you have, can help a person, a group, or a cause in need. You never know how your donation will help, so give early and give often.
- Create a financial plan. Your plan will be your road map to financial harmony and success. It'll guide you through good times and bad, up markets and down, work and retirement. It should include an investment policy statement and an income-distribution policy. With your plan you'll be able to track your progress and make changes as needed.
- Establish a sound asset-allocation policy. This will help diversify your investments across sectors and securities. Your asset-allocation policy will keep you diversified among large, small, and international companies as well bonds, cash, and alternative investments.
- Your financial plan and asset-allocation summary will determine your investment selection, which will determine your total return. The review of your investments should correspond with the review of your financial plan.

- The investments you own should be low cost. The lower your trading and investment costs, the better your returns will be. Individual investments and index funds will help keep a lid on your expenses.
- The income you receive should come from multiple sources inside your accounts. The income should come from most, if not all, of your holdings. Cash flow should also cross accounts—taxable and tax deferred. Diversified income will help preserve the longevity of your account.
- If you're over 70.5, you can use your required minimum distribution or RMD to help smooth your monthly cash flow. A monthly distribution from your IRA could help with budgeting as well. As I said earlier, the RMD isn't an income strategy but an income-*distribution* strategy. By receiving a monthly RMD check, it will allow your other investments to grow.
- Your estate offers a number of potential benefits from tax savings to higher income. Gifting some of your assets to others will help others in need.
- Work with an advisor who puts your interest first. It's your money, so work with someone who treats you well and honors your request.
- The model for investment and income success is simple: plan, invest, repeat.

Last, get outside and enjoy your retirement!

Bill Parrott is the founder and owner of Parrott Wealth Management. Bill started his investment career in May of 1989. During his career he has worked for Spelman & Company, Dean Witter Reynolds, Inc., Morgan Stanley, A.G. Edwards & Sons and Charles Schwab.

Bill earned his Bachelors of Business Administration from the University of San Diego in 1988. In 2003 he obtained the Certified Financial Planner designation.

Bill enjoys reading, running, fly-fishing and hiking. He lives in Austin, Texas with his wife and daughter.

www.parrottwealth.com

Made in the USA
Columbia, SC
02 May 2018